SOLD

on CHANGE!

Success Secrets of a
Top-Selling Real Estate Agent

OR

How to Recruit, Hire, and Train the Best Staff and Real Estate Agents, Create a Brokerage with an Effective Team Culture Focused on Winning, Utilize Technology and Develop Repeatable Systems to Ensure Success in the Housing Market

Bob Zachmeier

Out of the Box Books
Tucson, Arizona

This publication contains the opinions, ideas, and personal experiences of its author. It is sold with the understanding that neither the author nor the publisher is engaged in rendering legal, tax, investment, insurance, financial, accounting, or other professional advice or services. If the reader requires such advice or services, a competent professional should be consulted. Relevant laws vary from state to state. The strategies outlined in this book may not be suitable for every individual, and are not guaranteed or warranted to produce any particular results. No warranty is made with respect to the accuracy or completeness of the information contained herein, and both the author and the publisher specifically disclaim any responsibility for any liability, loss, or risk, personal or otherwise, which is incurred as a consequence, directly or indirectly, of the use and application of any of the contents of this book.

For information on other books by Bob Zachmeier
visit the publisher's website at:
www.outoftheboxbooks.com

When it comes to books… think Out of the Box!

Out of the Box Books
P.O. Box 64878, Tucson, AZ 85728

For Bill and BettyJo Zachmeier
I was blessed to have parents who expected great things from me.
Although my school grades may have disappointed them at times,
I feel that I now expect the same things from myself that they did.
Together, they gave me the confidence to set aggressive goals and
the discipline to achieve them.

"If you raise your children to feel that they can accomplish any goal or task they decide upon, you will have succeeded as a parent and you will have given your children the greatest of all blessings." – Brian Tracy

Table of Contents

TABLE OF CONTENTS

TABLE OF CONTENTS

TABLE OF CONTENTS

TABLE OF CONTENTS

<u>Figures in This Book</u>

TABLE OF CONTENTS

Change in Real Life (Actual Experiences)

ACKNOWLEDGEMENTS

This book was easy to write because I lived every minute of it over a three year period. I wrote this entire text in twenty-six days between five o'clock and eight o'clock in the morning!

In a world of uncertainty, I have never felt more richly blessed. I am surrounded by the best support group on earth!

I thank God for the love and support of my wife, Camille, who was awakened when I got up early to write or came to bed after a late night session of editing the manuscript.

I thank my parents. Dad taught me to see things as they *could be* rather than seeing them as they are. His *vision* and my Mom's optimism are alive and well in me today. Although my dad passed away in 1996, my mother is still actively experiencing life. She is sharp as ever and helped to proofread this book prior to printing.

I thank my brother, Mike, for quitting his job in an uncertain economy to relocate his family to Tucson and join our real estate business. He's worked hard to help us create a new division and he brings a different perspective to our business.

I thank Stuart Lott for enduring many late-night meetings to resolve challenges and track our progress. Stuart is the best organizer I've ever met. We would never have been able to achieve the sales volume we have without his strong work ethic, engineering skills, and tireless attitude.

I thank Robert Merideth, my editor and friend for fitting this project into a very hectic time in his life.

I thank John Harings for his friendship and loyalty. Although he sells over 100 homes per year, John attends every

ACKNOWLEDGEMENTS

agent meeting and is always fun to be around. He is an inspiration to the other agents in our company.

I thank Vanessa Chansky, who diligently converted my scribbled pages to the electronic text you are reading now.

I thank the agents and staff of Win3 Realty for their dedication and patience through our growing pains. A team is only as good as the sum of all of its players.

I thank our professional team including our accountant, Sean McCoy, our attorney, Jim Whitehill, and our escrow officer, Joann Bersell for their friendship and advice.

I thank Craig and Catherine Proctor. My view of real estate sales has been forever changed by their coaching program.

I thank Bryan Pellican for helping us get started in selling bank-owned properties. Our real estate business has achieved sales levels that we could never have imagined possible.

I thank Lester Cox in Tempe, AZ, Amy Coleman in Sacramento, CA, and Ian Reekie, in Portland, Oregon. I've formed close friendships with these real estate brokers and rarely go a week without speaking with them on the telephone or seeing them at a conference.

I thank Tom and Naomi Moon for creating a national network of caring people with a *Pay it Forward* attitude at www.reobroker.com. Their support of our fundraising endeavors for children's charities has made a huge difference in our community and is truly appreciated.

INTRODUCTION

The only thing that seems to stay constant is *change*. Each year, it seems to come faster and faster. In business, the companies that adapt to change the fastest win market share. Business owners who educate themselves to understand what is causing the change don't just survive; they *thrive!*

The Internet has turned local real estate into a global commodity. In the expanded world market, buyers can easily search for property in other cities, states, countries, and continents. Homeowners have the ability to conduct research, find recent sale data, and sell their property themselves on websites like www.ebay.com or www.zillow.com without using a real estate agent.

Many technically competent people believe that real estate agents have become obsolete because they no longer add value. In some ways, they are right, but as I will show you in this book, real estate agents capable of adapting to change can provide valuable services to their clients by finding creative ways to market their properties, invent programs that generate buying opportunities, and keep emotion out of negotiations.

By 2007, most US housing markets were in a steep decline. Foreclosures increased rapidly, especially in markets that had experienced rapid appreciation in the preceding years. Many areas in the desert southwest were among those hardest hit. These "sand states" include Arizona, California, and Nevada. As the owner of a real estate brokerage in Tucson,

INTRODUCTION

Arizona, I have had to change the way we do business as home prices and the number of sales declined drastically.

A popular advertising campaign states that, "What happens in Vegas stays in Vegas," but that is not true. In reality, most real estate market changes originate in Los Angeles before "happening" in Las Vegas. Next, they continue eastward to Phoenix and then south to Tucson. Because changes in other markets affect my market, I regularly attend real estate conferences to stay abreast of what is happening in other areas of the country, especially in other "sand states."

We have constantly adjusted our business as the market changed around us. We sold six homes per month in 2007, an all-time high for us. From 2008 to 2010, as other real estate agents watched their sales steadily decline, our sales increased by 1,000%! By 2010, we were closing *sixty* homes per month, ten times more than the all-time high we had achieved just three years earlier.

Our success is due to our willingness to change our practices to adapt to the market. I am convinced that if we stopped making changes we would be out of business within two years. Although it does not come naturally, I have learned to *embrace* change.

We can no longer expect to work at a job for thirty or forty years like our parents. Many jobs in the workplace today will not even exist five years from now. New technology is changing the world around us almost daily. We must constantly adapt in order to survive.

INTRODUCTION

Our business prospered because we hired and trained good employees to complete many tasks, created repeatable systems to ensure consistent results, and utilized technology whenever it becomes available. We constantly track local and national housing trends as well as data in our own company. In addition, we consult regularly with coaches and colleagues around the country who are willing to share their wisdom, advice, and keys to their success.

I organized this book as follows: Chapters 1-4 discuss our progression through coaching and declining commissions. Chapters 4-8 discuss recruiting, hiring, compensating and training employees and creating company culture. Chapters 9-12 discuss how to divide your business into divisions, which numbers to track and which work to delegate. Chapters 13-18 discuss how we use inside sales staff to screen calls and book appointments as well as how to recruit, train, and compensate agents. Chapters 19-22 discuss the organization of our REO and short sale divisions. Chapters 23-25 discuss technology that will make your business more efficient. Chapters 26-28 discuss ways to advertise and get referrals from the people you know. Chapters 29-31 discuss sharing.

This book will help anyone in Sales establish systems, recognize change, and adapt quickly, just as we have. Many people share their successes, but you can learn a lot more from their failures. Throughout this book, I've shared many ideas that have worked, but also things that *didn't* work. Knowing what doesn't work should help you achieve results faster than we did and you will soon be on the fast track to success.

1

Forging Our Future

The transition from a corporate job at Raytheon to opening our own brokerage

"The future belongs to those who believe in the beauty of their dreams."– Eleanor Roosevelt

SOLD ON CHANGE!

In October 1998, a series of events began to unfold that would significantly alter my destiny and that of my fiancée, Camille. At the time, we were busily making plans for our wedding when Raytheon notified us that the defense plant where we both worked in Lewisville, Texas was closing.

Raytheon had purchased the Defense Electronics division of Texas Instruments, and six months later bought Hughes Electronics. Several manufacturing plants around the country were consolidated in Tucson, Arizona. Raytheon offered us a job there and scheduled our move to Tucson just three weeks after our wedding. This would give us just enough time to unpack from our honeymoon and oversee the movers.

Within a month of receiving the notification, we purchased a beautiful home on a golf course in Tucson. We had amazing mountain views, a sparkling pool and lush citrus trees loaded with fruit (a novelty for me, a North Dakota native). We were excited about our new life together in Arizona and everything seemed to be going our way.

We loved living in Tucson, but hated our new jobs so we began purchasing, fixing up, and renting out homes near the University of Arizona. After purchasing several properties, we decided that it would be advantageous to obtain our real estate licenses. We took the required classes in the evenings after work and passed the test in May 2000.

During our first year as real estate agents, we exceeded the industry average by selling three homes in seven months, but two of the homes we purchased ourselves. In 2001, we sold ten homes, seven to clients and three to ourselves.

In 2002, Camille and I sold 25 homes in our spare time while working ten-hour days at Raytheon and driving an hour each way to work. We rarely commuted together because I always seemed to have a home inspection scheduled over lunch or a client appointment after work. We were both driving 75 miles round trip to work each day and something had to change.

In June 2002, at the age of 42, I quit my job. After 22 years of a steady paycheck, my dependence on corporate America was over. Quitting my job is still the scariest thing I've ever done, but we had saved well and were earning a significant amount of income from our rental properties.

My boss asked me to stay long enough to complete a critical project, so I worked ten-hour days on Tuesdays and Thursdays for the next six months. On January 8, 2003, I walked out of Raytheon for the last time. After so many years of working with analytical engineers, it was nice to be able to carry on friendly conversations with everyone I met. In a defense plant, you do not discuss anything unless others have a "need to know."

I enjoyed my new career and was able to put my technical skills to use by analyzing real estate market data. I created charts to educate my clients about the seasonal trends in our local market.

To attract clients, I began teaching real estate classes for novice investors at Pima Community College in 2001. Word spread quickly about my classes and enrollments continually increased. Within a year, I was teaching eight six-week classes per year. The students who took my classes became motivated after learning the basics of real estate investment and soon turned into a steady stream of real estate clients.

In 2003, I sold 31 homes while Camille continued to work full-time at Raytheon. By January 2004, I was so busy that I could no longer keep up, so I went back to Raytheon one last time to get Camille. It was her birthday, so I filled a limousine with friends and family and we picked her up from work in style. Her birthday present was that she did not have to go back to Raytheon anymore! After 20 years, she was out of the "rat race" too!

Three months later, after being with the same real estate broker for four years, we decided it was time to launch our own brokerage. We needed a name that was long enough to describe the service we provided but short enough to fit inexpensively in classified ads. We chose *Win3 Realty* because it reflects our win-win-win philosophy where the clients win, the company wins, and the community wins. When we first opened our doors, many people thought our name was *Winfrey Realty* (like Oprah), but today, with over three hundred listed properties and signs in the ground across our market area, most agents in Tucson know who we are.

Shortly after starting our new company, we learned that the lender we had been using for several years had been charging our clients fees that were much higher than normal. This prompted Camille to take lending classes to become a loan officer. She began generating the mortgages for many of our clients to ensure that they received fair treatment and that their loans would fund on time. This allowed us to become a "one stop shop" for many of our clients who needed to be pre-qualified after normal business hours. Even with the diversions of starting a new real estate company and a loan business, we managed to sell 43 homes in 2004.

By June 2005, our businesses had taken over our lives. We were selling a home every week, but we were so busy we had to turn clients away. We were always exhausted and seemed surrounded by chaos. Working harder was not possible so we had to find a way to work *smarter*.

Camille read about a real estate "SuperConference" being held in Phoenix by a real estate agent from Canada who had systemized his business. We registered to go and our lives have not been the same since.

2

Coaching with Craig

How Craig Proctor's coaching helped our real estate business take a Quantum Leap

"Give a man a fish and you feed him for a day. Teach him how to fish and you feed him for a lifetime."– Lao Tzu

At the conference, we learned that Craig Proctor was a real estate agent in New Market, Ontario, about an hour north of Toronto. He had left his job as a hospital janitor to follow his father as a real estate agent. When he arrived at work the first day, someone handed him a telephone book and said, "Start calling."

Craig found that he was very good at sales but soon became exhausted in the time-consuming sales process. He, like us, had reached his maximum output and was killing himself trying to do everything alone. With help from Jay Abraham, Michael Gerber, and Dan Kennedy, he learned to utilize people, technology, and systems to put much of the time-consuming work on autopilot.

At the age of 26, he had become the number one selling RE/Max agent in the world and had remained in the top 10 worldwide since then. At the time of the Phoenix conference, he was selling over 500 homes per year, which is amazing because he lived in a town of only 75,000 people.

We were killing ourselves to sell 50 homes; how could anyone sell 500? Could this be true? During the next two and a half days, we learned how he sold so many homes. The innovation was amazing! By the first two hours, I had several pages of notes and could not wait to get home to start implementing some of the new things we had already learned. By the end of the conference, I was angry with myself for having wasted five years doing business the hard way.

CHAPTER 2 – COACHING WITH CRAIG

Camille wanted to sign up for their coaching program, but I felt certain that I could implement many of the things we had learned by ourselves. Finally, she reasoned with me that the cost of having a coach for a year was less than we'd earn from two commission checks. So I relented and we signed up for coaching. How could we <u>not</u> sell two additional homes per year with someone so successful coaching us? That decision changed our lives.

Our first order of business was to hire support staff for our office. We ran the ad and followed the hiring procedures our coach recommended and received 146 resumes in the first week. We reviewed the work history and experience of each candidate and invited 18 people for an interview.

We divided the candidates into three groups and set up one-hour sessions for each group in our title company's conference room. After giving a brief description of the culture we intended to create, we asked the applicants to complete a personality profile.

The coaching was already helping us be more effective and leverage our time. We had attracted an unbelievable number of applicants, screened them, and hired the best candidate in just *five hours!* The employee we hired, Marianne Kartsonis, is still with us today. The system worked!

In the previous five years, Camille and I had never been able to get more than eight transactions under contract at one time. The three times we had achieved that mark, we had to stop selling to ensure that each transaction closed on time. This caused our sales for the following month to suffer and we would have only one or two closings. Our sales were sporadic and looked much like the oscillating graph of a heart rate monitor but, after eighteen months of coaching, we were averaging eight sales <u>every</u> month!

We sold 63 homes in 2005 and increased the total to 65 in 2006 while we trained new staff members and began incorporating more systems into our business. What is not apparent from the numbers is that we were no longer doing all of the work. We were able to work less and take vacations again. We sold 80 homes in 2007, more than we sold in our first *four years* as real estate agents! The training was really beginning to pay off.

In 2007, at a SuperConference in Denver, Bryan Pellican, a fellow coaching member from Las Vegas, Nevada, shared how he had begun to sell foreclosed homes for banks. He helped us create a resume and showed us how to apply with various banks. Two banks hired us within a month of the conference and within eighteen months, we were selling homes for 17 financial institutions in addition to our existing real estate sales.

We ended 2008 with 285 closings; more than *triple* the amount we had achieved in 2007. Three years after making the decision to sign up for coaching, we had increased our sales by nearly 500%. We received the exclusive Quantum Leap award for achieving the most exceptional growth among the thousands of agents being coached in the program.

CHAPTER 2 – COACHING WITH CRAIG

In 2009, we drastically increased our residential sales when my brother, Mike, joined our company. Mike was the Director of Quality at a General Electric subsidiary in Boulder, Colorado and felt that his career had stagnated. After several discussions with Mike and his wife, Carla, he decided to quit the high-paying job that he didn't enjoy and move to Tucson. Trading a secure paycheck for the uncertainty of a real estate career in a slow economy is a bold move. In hindsight, I should have hired a limousine for him too!

Mike moved his family to Tucson, enrolled the kids in school, and was selling homes within a few months of making his initial visit. Mike is a natural salesperson. He had his license less than 24 hours before making his first sale. With the systems we had in place, he was able to sell more in his first nine months than Camille and I sold during our first *two years* as agents. This feat is even more impressive when you consider that he did not know the area and had no personal acquaintances.

We embarked on a deliberate course to implement more systems, do a better job of tracking the results, and make changes where necessary to improve our business. After three years of constant growth, we were only utilizing about 25% of the marketing materials and systems that were available to us through our coaching program.

When Camille and I had first listened to the bi-weekly coaching calls, we did not have a team to help us implement the new ideas and systems. The few systems we implemented had worked so well that we were too busy to implement more. I was determined to do better the second time around.

A new coaching group was starting for the agents who had joined the program at the previous conference. To ensure better results than Camille and I produced by ourselves, we hired Amy Randall to be our full-time marketing manager, Vanessa Hillman as our full-time call coordinator, and my brother, Mike, to oversee the department and coach the sales agents with his obvious skill.

This was to be a one-year experiment. The goal was to have Mike get on the coaching calls every two weeks and implement whatever new system was introduced before the next coaching call two weeks later. Did we succeed in implementing all of the systems available? No! Within a few months, we had fallen behind *again!* Even three people working full time could not implement in one year what had taken Craig Proctor 15 years to perfect.

Although we did not get all of the systems in place, we were able to add another 25% of the material to our arsenal. The biggest accomplishment of this effort was getting our team members to share the vision we had for our company. When a group focuses on the same goal, everyone understands where their responsibilities start and end. When you regularly track your progress, the goal will become a reality very quickly.

On September 15, 2009, our team surpassed the Tucson market's all-time MLS record for the most sales in one calendar year. We did it with 101 days left in the year. Although this record is nice to own, I am more proud of the fact that we have brought more buyers to the closing table for the past three years than any other agent or team in our market.

Were the results worth the expense of three additional employees? Our one-year experiment produced 45 *additional* sales during the first half of the year and 99 more during the second half. We ended 2009 with 144 closings from our newly-formed Residential Division and 502 sales overall, a substantial increase over the 285 homes we had sold the previous year. Would you like to deposit 217 more commission checks in your bank account next year? Hire some good employees or hard-working family members and a coach to show you how!

After five years of striving to achieve Craig Proctor's level of success, I feel safe in saying that we finally made it! However, because of the increasing demand for homes in the Tucson market, and the high productivity of our sales team, we should be able to sell far more homes than we are currently selling.

Although we are smashing previous sales records, we sell only 2% of all homes sold in our MLS. This is very good news because it means we have a long way to go before we reach market saturation.

For 2010, our Residential Sales team set a goal of 25 sales per month. A key point here is that I didn't set the goal, the team did. If we were able to meet our goal, the Residential Division would contribute 300 sales to the overall total. Typically, sales in the first quarter are substantially lower than at any other time in the year.

SOLD ON CHANGE!

Even so, we were on target to achieve our goal by mid-year. We closed two homes per *day* for much of the year; an average real estate agent sells only two homes all *year!*

3

Plummeting Profits
The effect of lower sale prices and lower commissions on our bottom line

"Rule Number One: Never lose money. Rule Number Two: Never forget rule Number One." – Warren Buffett

SOLD ON CHANGE!

As it turned out, even though we sold three times more homes in 2008 than we did in 2007, our profit was lower. We needed to figure out whether our decline in profit was due to lower income or higher expenses.

Often when there is a money problem, a person's first reaction is to reduce expenses. However, if the falling profit stems from a loss of income, reducing expenses will not solve the problem. The more homes you sell the more people you will need to employ. By cutting back on employees, you will reduce the amount of your payroll but it will also reduce the number of homes you are able to sell, which will lead to an even further reduction of income. To overcome a reduction of income you must increase volume and improve efficiency.

The average sale price of the homes we sold was about $166,000 in 2008, which on average was $61,500 lower than the previous year! If you assume that we earned a 3% commission during both years, we would have received $1,850 *less* for each home sold in 2008 than we earned in 2007. We definitely had experienced a reduction in our income!

When multiplied by the 285 homes sold in 2008, our income was $526,000 *less* than we would have earned by selling the same number of homes the previous year! The reason for the large drop in our average sale price was partially due to the market, but also because we spent too much of our marketing effort focusing on foreclosure properties. The average sale price of foreclosed homes fell much further than the average sale price overall.

CHAPTER 3 – PLUMMETING PROFITS

In 2008, foreclosed home sales represented 85% of our overall business. We set out to change that by increasing residential sales to families, rental property sales to investors, and short sales for people unable to sell because their mortgage is higher than the value of their home. Within eighteen months, foreclosed home sales represented less than 50% of our overall sales. We did not reduce the number of foreclosure sales; in fact, we added several new bank clients in 2009 and 2010. The ratio dropped due to significant increases in the number of residential, investor, and short sale transactions we completed.

Home values continued to fall by about $500 per week on average. Many people were losing more on their home each day than they earned working at their job! By the end of 2009, the average price of the homes we sold had fallen to just over $139,000, a drop of another $26,500 in home value and a related drop in commission of nearly $800 per sale from the previous year. In only two years, the amount we earned for selling each home decreased by nearly $2,700, a reduction of 40%. Most people would be unable to deal with a 40% pay cut, but we had to find a way to absorb the loss.

The US government attempted to stabilize home prices and stimulate the real estate market in 2009 by introducing tax credits, down payment assistance programs, and low-interest loans. In addition to these buyer incentives, the supply of foreclosed homes on the market mysteriously declined during this time. The increased demand and reduced supply led to multiple offers on many homes in the lower end of the market range.

SOLD ON CHANGE!

The bidding wars drove home prices temporarily higher but when the stimulus programs ended, the market stopped abruptly. In April 2010, our office received 85 offers per week, an average of five offers for every home we sold. Immediately after the deadline passed for an $8,000 tax credit, the number of new offers we received fell to only 27 per week. The stimulus did not create more buyers; it just caused them to act sooner than they normally might have in the absence of incentives.

Our average sale price fell sharply to $102,000, down more than $37,000 from the previous year and $125,500 over the previous three years. We continued to find creative ways to cut expenses and increase income in order to absorb a loss of nearly $3,800 on every home sold. When multiplied by the 800 homes we expect to sell in 2010, our gross income is $3.0 million *lower* than it would have been if we had sold the same number of homes in 2007.

To increase commissions, we created advertising and programs that would produce higher value sales. We could not sustain another loss of $1,000 per sale; the margins were just too thin. We had been able to compensate for lower and lower commissions during the previous three years by selling 200 additional homes each year. But increasing the volume only works if there is *profit*.

When you spend more than your earn, increasing your volume only makes you lose more money. I theorized that by attracting better agents to sell regular residential properties (i.e., not bank-owned, or REO, properties) and by increasing the number of short sales we handled, we could close more sales at or near the overall MLS market average of $160,000 rather than the MLS average of $115,000 for bank-owned properties.

4

Predicting Personality
How personality testing can influence the way you recruit and hire employees

"My father always told me, "Find a job you love and you'll never have to work a day in your life."– Jim Fox

Licensing courses at real estate schools teach you how to pass the state's test to obtain a license, but they do not teach you how to become a successful agent or how to build an effective team. So how do you find good agents and staff? Do you look for experienced agents that are already successful or rookies who are new and hungry?

Throughout the book, I provide as much detail as possible about the people we recruit and hire for various positions in our company. No matter which position we are interviewing for, the two qualities that we look for above all else are work ethic and loyalty. These are traits that cannot be taught, people either have them or they don't.

Most real estate "teams" do not really function as a team, they consist of several agents who share one or two administrative assistants. Can you imagine a professional baseball team with pitchers playing all nine positions? Although being able to throw well is important, in the game of baseball your team also must be able to hit, run, and catch.

Effective teams consist of a diverse group of people who have different skill sets and experiences. Because each team member performs the same task on every transaction, they become an expert at their job and develop checklists and shortcuts to become more efficient than someone who only does the job occasionally.

To make automobiles more affordable, Henry Ford developed an assembly line. Each employee completed a specific set of clearly defined tasks before another team member performed their tasks. Each member of an efficient team must know exactly where their duties start and end.

For example, our Advertising Department has responsibility of making potential clients "raise their hand" in response to our selling propositions. We measure the effectiveness of our advertising by the number of unique client contacts we receive via telephone calls, e-mail, and website inquiries.

These inquiries come to our Inside Sales Department, which is responsible for converting the inquiries into appointments for our agents. The inside sales associate educates the potential clients about the benefits we can provide for them. We measure the effectiveness of our lead conversion team by the number of times a potential client walks into our office for a meeting with an agent.

The licensed real estate agents in our Outside Sales Department are responsible for meeting with the prospective clients, determining their needs, and winning their business by demonstrating that we have the experience, knowledge, and resources to deliver what they are looking for. We measure the effectiveness of each outside sales agent by the number of signed agreements produced, the number of offers they write or receive, and the number of transactions they close.

We closely track each aspect of the transaction from the first phone call to the closing and follow up months and years after the sale. Members of our team know exactly where their duties start and stop and where the next person takes over.

DISC Personality Profile

Potential agents and staff members who pass our initial scrutiny are required to complete a DISC personality profile. DISC is a four quadrant behavioral model based on the work of William Moulton Marston in the 1920s. The DISC personality profile consists of 24 questions that examine a person's behavior to determine their dominant preferences and personality style.

Each personality style brings a unique value to a team so we utilize this tool to determine the general characteristics and preferred working environment of each person we interview. DISC is an acronym for **D**ominance, **I**nfluence, **S**teadiness, and **C**ompliance. The common traits of each personality type are below:

Dominant – Personality traits include: driving, determined, aggressive, ambitious, and forceful. An example of a "D" personality would be an *Army General*.

Influential – Personality traits include: persuasive, warm, optimistic, emotional, and demonstrative. An example of an "I" personality would be a *Sales Person*.

Steady – Personality traits include: calm, relaxed, patient, possessive, predictable, and consistent. An example of an "S" personality would be a *Social Worker*.

Compliant – Personality traits include: careful, cautious, neat, systematic, and structured. An example of a "C" personality would be an *Accountant*.

Change in Real Life

It's A Small World

Although there are more than three million people in the United States, on occasion you will find someone who knows someone you know in another part of the country.

My friend, Aaron Kinn, in Dallas, TX created a Microsoft Excel file that we send anonymously to job applicants. Aaron's name was in the "Properties" section as the creator of the file and one applicant who made it through our initial screening not only noticed the name, he *knew* Aaron Kinn!

He called Aaron to ask why a file created in Texas was being used to qualify him for a job in Arizona. Aaron explained that we had been in Craig Proctor's coaching program together for many years and that he had shared his file with others in our group.

The applicant was Colin Penny and we hired him. Colin has turned out to be a reliable employee. The fact that he caught this minute detail showed us that he possesses the attention to detail that we were seeking! You just never know when you will meet someone who knows other people in your life.

5

Analyzing Applicants

How to advertise, interview, and test the skill of employees before you hire them

"There are three ways to get something done: do it yourself, employ someone, or forbid your children to do it."
– Monta Crane

When you need to hire help, it's a good idea to create a list of all the tasks the new employees will perform so you will know in advance the personality type of the employee that would be best equipped to handle the job.

Before we advertise for new team members, we develop a job description with a list of the duties to be performed, a list of the minimum skills and experience required, the hours of the day when an employee would need to be available, and an expectation of how long it should take to complete each task.

We use the following steps to determine the type of employee we need. Without knowing the skills and experience level you require, you will not know where to advertise to attract the applicants that best match your criteria.

1) Map the entire process from beginning to end.
2) Develop a job description for each task in the process.
3) Determine the DISC personality type (see previous chapter) that would best fit each job.
4) Determine the skill level and experience necessary for the job.
5) Estimate the time required to complete each task in the process.
6) Determine the compensation you can afford to pay for each task and how important it is to the business.
7) Determine the capacity limit at which another employee would be required.
8) Determine how to divide the tasks if you hired two employees.

9) Set a threshold at which to add and train additional staff. Be sure to allow enough time to recruit, hire, and train before reaching capacity.

Nearly all of the tasks in our main office are repetitive and detail-oriented. Employees who enjoy work like this are usually very reliable and make few mistakes.

In a real estate transaction, a simple mistake can cost thousands of dollars. The biggest fear of detail-oriented people is to be *wrong* so they often double and triple check the accuracy of their work, which protects our company, and more importantly, our clients.

When we have a need for an employee who is computer literate and a fast typist, we run the ad in Figure 5-1 on www.craigslist.com.

We usually get more than twenty replies to our generic e-mail account every time we post this ad. We sort the e-mails by subject line and delete the applications from those who did not type the exact code in the subject line of their e-mail. The text in the subject line code is meaningless, but it works great to determine whether applicants are detail-oriented. We don't waste time interviewing applicants who cannot follow directions.

We review each applicant's job experience and cover letter to determine whether their experience would benefit our team. We also scan each application for spelling errors, poor grammar, and overall neatness. Because it takes so long to train employees, applicants who do not have a steady work history are not considered.

Figure 5-1 Craigslist Computer Geek Ad

Computer GEEK (Market Analyst) (Tucson, Arizona)

Summary:

The successful candidate will provide an accurate opinion of value for homes in the Tucson area based on past sales and properties that are currently available for sale.

Responsibilities:

Run comparative market analysis on properties in the Multiple Listing Service (MLS)
Analyze the MLS data gathered and establish the price point at which a property will sell
Enter findings into predefined data fields quickly and accurately
Upload the information to vendor websites

Requirements:

Self-starter (although our pay possibilities will motivate you!).
Good math and analytical skills
Ability to type 100 words per minute with good accuracy and spelling
Experience using Microsoft Excel
Comprehensive understanding of averaging and calculating medians

This role requires a strong aptitude for math and analytical skills and the ability to upload information into predefined fields quickly. Speed and accuracy are of utmost importance.

E-mail resume and cover letter to XXXX@gmail.com
Place "CODE: F53627Y" (without quotes) in the subject line

- Location: Tucson, Arizona
- Compensation: Base pay plus piecework bonus (up to $50/hour!)
- Principals only. No recruiters.
- Phone calls about this job are not ok, FAX only.
- Please do not contact about other services, products or commercial interests.

We e-mail the DISC personality profile to promising applicants and chart the results of those who completed the profile correctly to determine whether their respective personality types match the position we have available. We contact applicants who have the desired skills, experience, and personality via telephone for an interview. Those who use good grammar, enunciate clearly, and can carry on a conversation in a professional manner are invited for a face-to-face interview at our office.

Upon receiving the invitation for an interview, the applicants learn whom they have been communicating with during the application process. Applicants disqualified for one reason or another never know who we are. Our screening process usually thins the field of applicants by 75% or more. This makes sense because there are four personality types and we have specifically sought to hire an employee with the characteristics of one personality type.

We intentionally schedule the interviews back-to-back so applicants will see the other applicants and know that there is a huge demand for the position we have available. We seat the applicants at a computer when they arrive and ask them to verify the skills listed on their resume.

We first check the speed and accuracy of their typing by using the online test at www.typingtest.com. Next we test their basic and advanced knowledge of Microsoft Excel. Every department in our company uses Excel to track its output, so it's crucial to find employees who can use the program proficiently.

After completing the typing test and the Excel test on the computer, we seat the applicants in our conference room. Those conducting the interview receive copies of each applicant's resume, cover letter, DISC personality concept, typing test, and Excel test.

Our office manager and the department manager usually conduct the interviews. If the new position will require working closely with others on the team, those employees also attend the interview to provide feedback on each applicant.

The interviews typically last 15 to 20 minutes and always start with a description of our company culture and the team atmosphere that causes our team to perform so well. We then allow the applicant to tell us whether they are interested in the position we have available, and if so, why they think they would be a good fit with our company.

We ask them to identify specific things they liked and disliked about their previous jobs and to elaborate on how their experience could benefit our company.

After the interviews, we rank the candidates and notify them of our decision. On several occasions we have hired two candidates who interviewed strongly when we only had one opening. While it costs more to do so, our reasoning is that people are your most important asset and you cannot allow good ones to get away! New opportunities always present themselves and you need to have the staff available to capitalize on these opportunities when they come.

6

Hiring Help

How to create job descriptions and know when to add additional staff

"The secret of getting started is breaking your complex overwhelming tasks into small manageable tasks, and then starting on the first one."– Mark Twain

In this chapter, I have laid out the step-by-step process of how we added employees and split tasks as our business grew from zero employees in 2005 to more than thirty employees in 2010.

Personal Assistant- The first person to hire is a personal assistant. The person you hire for this position should be well organized and able to multi-task without becoming unduly stressed. The person should have the organizational qualities of a "C" personality type but also possess some "I" or "S" tendencies to be flexible and friendly on the telephone.

The main task of this person is to stop the barrage of unnecessary interruptions that affect your productivity. You should avoid spending your time on tasks if you cannot change the outcome! The personal assistant you hire should immediately begin answering the telephone and responding to e-mails that do not require your intervention. You may need to redirect personal e-mails that you would not want an employee to see.

A good assistant will enable you to spend less time on mundane tasks and more time creating new business for your company. The additional income that you generate should easily be enough to justify the expense of the additional staff member. You should delegate any clerical or administrative task that does not require your expertise to your assistant. Disorganized areas of your office will mysteriously become orderly within a few weeks of hiring an effective assistant.

CHAPTER 6 – HIRING HELP

We waited far too long to hire someone to help with clerical tasks and organizing our office. On her first day, Marianne Kartsonis was typing, faxing, and filing everything in sight. Within a week, we had developed a smooth system, except for the way we handled phone calls.

Marianne would energetically answer the phone and greet each caller like a long-lost friend. She was friendly, professional, and everyone loved her, but the callers would always ask to speak with me. I asked Marianne to see how many of the callers she could assist without transferring them to me. I could detect hesitation and uneasiness in her voice. She could not tell callers I was gone when I was sitting three feet away from her so she would usually end up placing them on hold and transferring them to me.

I did not expect Marianne to lie to the callers, but I really needed them to allow her to help them. Finally, I came up with a solution. I retrieved our label maker and printed a label that read "the phone." I stuck it on the leg of my chair and informed Marianne that I had named my chair. Now when she told anyone who called that I was on "the phone" it would be true!

It took a while to get some of the clients and agents who'd always spoken with me in the past to deal with Marianne. Some callers would refuse to reveal the purpose of their call and simply leave a message for me to call them back. When I'd return their call I'd often find that what they needed easily could have been provided by Marianne.

SOLD ON CHANGE!

One day I realized that by giving personal attention to those who would not disclose the reason for their call, I was inadvertently encouraging them to bypass Marianne. I began to contact them, determine what they wanted, and then would transfer them back to Marianne. Once they found out that they could not bypass Marianne to get to me, they stopped asking for me.

I had always handled every aspect of my transactions myself and was very concerned about how our clients would feel about me delegating parts of the process to Marianne. I modified our buyer and seller presentations to explain to our clients the reasons we had changed.

The presentation for sellers explained that if I spent my time doing all of the clerical tasks I would not have time to create marketing campaigns for their home. The presentation for buyers explained how I would be unable to find the perfect home for them if I was constantly on the phone.

The presentations worked. We started selling more homes and our team grew quickly. We educated new clients about our team system upfront and told them they would receive the services of our entire staff for less than some agents charged for only one person.

Soon our clients were dealing with our staff every day and I was able to concentrate on selling more homes. One day I answered the phone when our employees were on other lines. The caller was one of my clients, but he asked to speak with

CHAPTER 6 – HIRING HELP

Marianne! I placed him on hold and went back to what I was doing. I knew then that our team system was working!

Marianne is my gatekeeper and has been on a mission to protect my time since 2005. She has saved me from thousands of unnecessary interruptions by obtaining the necessary information and either transferring the call to another member of our staff or resolving the issue herself. I rarely receive more than ten calls per week that our staff cannot handle.

A good assistant will allow you to take your business to the next level by handling situations that don't require your attention. For example, you should never even know that Page 2 of the fax did not go through, your assistant will just handle it, freeing up your time to create more business.

The person you hire should be organized, friendly, efficient, and smart. They should be strong in the areas where you are weak and unafraid to nudge you politely with reminders to complete tasks or make the unpleasant phone calls that many brokers tend to avoid.

Use the TimeTracker™ (available on my website at www.soldonchange.com) to determine which tasks you should delegate to your assistant. As your business grows, you will need to repeat the exercise at least once per quarter to continually free up more time to work on your business rather than in your business.

Working on your business involves delegating tasks that don't require your expertise to others on your team. Time not spent on day-to-day tasks can be used to create new advertising campaigns, attend training classes and conferences, or network with other business owners. Rather than wasting time on situations in which you cannot change the outcome, use your time to develop new business relationships and improve processes to become more efficient and productive.

Block your time to reserve at least five hours per week to work on your business. How much additional income could you generate if you spent twenty hours per month to educate yourself and generate new ideas? Could you sell two more homes each month? If so, you would sell 24 more homes per year, which could potentially add more than $100,000 to your annual income - an *awesome* return on an investment of only five hours per week!

As our team grew, I was able to delegate more day-to-day activities to our agents and staff. For the past two years, I have been working on our business far more than I work in it. We have been able to add at least 200 additional home sales in each of the past 3 years. Working smarter *works!*

When you have created and perfected a new process, you must delegate it to someone else who will keep it working. The longer you do it yourself, the longer it will take to turn the next idea into reality. Create, perfect, delegate!

As your business grows, you will need to hire and train more people to help keep up with the ever-growing number of phone calls, e-mails, and opportunities. On the following pages

I have provided a description of the positions we created and the order in which we staffed them.

<u>Property Specialist (Listing Department)</u> - Real estate agents are the only people who refer to someone's home as a "listing." We try to avoid using the "L" word when referring to our client's properties. We prefer to use the word "property" instead.

When you have several properties listed for sale, you will need to hire someone to ensure that the data and photos appear on the Multiple Listing Service (MLS) website in a timely manner so the property is included in searches conducted by potential buyers or their agents. We also double-check to ensure that all paperwork is accurate and complete. Paula Lipsitz has managed this area for us since 2006.

The people hired for this position should have a "C" personality type because of the accuracy required in getting the correct information about the property. They will also need to be able to communicate clearly with our clients, sign companies, couriers who visit the properties, and other agents who call with questions.

Staff members in this department coordinate sign installation, assign the appropriate sign riders, make key copies, and arrange for key safe installation on the home before the property becomes active on the MLS. After a property becomes active, they track the showing activity and provide our clients with feedback from the agents who have previewed or shown the property.

Every three weeks the property specialists run a new competitive market analysis and send it to our clients to show new homes in the area that have recently been listed for sale and information about any that have been sold. This keeps our clients aware of how many similar homes are for sale in their neighborhood, the asking price of the competing homes, and how much the homes that sell are fetching.

When our clients decide to make price adjustments, the property specialist prepares the paperwork, coordinates with the client to obtain their signature and makes the necessary adjustments online and in our marketing materials. This is easier and more efficient than trying to track down their agent, who may not be near a computer.

Offer Specialist (Offer Department) - The Offer Specialists in our main office are responsible for receiving and tracking all offers sent or received by our team. The Offer Department maintains a timeline for each offer under consideration and reviews their spreadsheet daily to ensure that agents and clients meet the deadlines.

The Offer Department receives all offers, forwards them to other agents and their clients, files them, and assigns a tracking number that complies with the state Department of Real Estate requirements. Offers remain the responsibility of this department until they are accepted, rejected, or expire. Marianne Kartsonis has done this for us since 2005.

Transaction Specialist (Closing Coordinator) - When phone calls, e-mails and problem solving becomes a full-time job to keep transactions on track, you will need to hire a transaction coordinator. This person is responsible for ensuring that everything is complete so the sale can close on schedule. This person should be organized and thorough but must be able to dial up the "D" in their personality to be very firm with lackadaisical lenders in order to meet performance deadlines.

We use a thirty-four item checklist for each transaction to ensure that everything happens in a timely manner. We often maintain more than three hundred active files, so we developed a system that enables us to find documents quickly and easily. Sam Andes has managed the licensed and unlicensed staff members in this department since 2008.

The files are stored in alphabetical order by property address and each file contains six separate tabs for listing information, contract documents, lead-based paint and seller disclosures, title company correspondence, miscellaneous information, and a communication history of fax and e-mail records. We review each transaction every two to three days to ensure that deadlines are not missed and to avoid unexpected issues at closing.

Hiring College Students

My friend Lester Cox, the owner/broker of Pacific Arizona Realty in Tempe, AZ, has encouraged many agents in our group to hire college interns to do administrative work. Lester tends to hire juniors and seniors who can work at least 30 hours or more per week while maintaining their studies. Many college students *need* a job to pay for their school-related expenses. As a result, they often work harder than many full-time employees do.

We have three college students working in our office. We do not have the desk space for employees to work fewer than 30 hours per week, so that's what they must commit to. We allow them to work around their school schedules with more hours over the summer and fewer during final exams. We have found that most student employees learn very quickly. We train them in several areas of the business so they can fill in easily when a department falls behind.

Change in Real Life

Students Taking Charge

I walked by our transaction department the other day and overheard Melissa Benjamin, one of our student employees, asking a lender why he had lied about the status of a loan and why he wasn't performing as promised.

She informed the lender that he was now on our *"Wall of Shame"* and that we would inform future clients that his loan approval letter is worthless because he is a lender who has a history of over-promising and under-delivering.

I could not help but smile. When we hired Melissa nine months earlier, she was very timid and you could barely hear her on the telephone. Welcome to life in the business world! The job ownership that our student employees have taken is AWESOME!

Their employment started with the students needing a job to help pay for school, but due to the bleak job market, some of our student employees have expressed an interest in continuing their employment with us after graduation.

Bret Johnson, an intern that Lester hired started as a transaction coordinator, which was a great way for him to learn the real estate business. When he graduated from college, he obtained his real estate licensed and soon became the top-selling agent in the office. He is now in training to take over the business when Lester retires.

By posting ads at your local college or university, you will find employees who *need* jobs, are intelligent, and very dependable. Most students who work their way through college are motivated and learn quickly. They tend to be very computer literate so you do not have to spend time or money on computer training.

We pay the students the same wage as our full-time employees. We have been very pleased with the character and work ethic of most of the students we have hired!

7

Empowering Employees

Pay structures that encourage employees to make decisions and maximize profits

"The difference between involvement and commitment is like ham and eggs. The chicken is involved; the pig is committed."
– Martina Navratilova

We meet weekly to review the workload for each department. If someone is on vacation or the department employees have to work too late to keep up, we make decisions on whether to shift employees from one department to another or hire someone new.

Every two weeks we review our income and expenses so we can determine whether we can afford to hire new employees. We calculate our profit or loss each month and pay employee bonuses if we achieve certain earning thresholds each quarter.

I would recommend a bonus structure based on *profit* rather than one based on income. For example, we pay our Operations Manager a monthly salary to handle most day-to-day staffing issues. But, in addition to his salary, he also earns a percentage of the company's overall profit.

I know several brokers who pay a flat fee to their employees based on each property closing. Although this is legal with staff members who hold a real estate license, paying an unlicensed staff member based on the outcome of a sale is not legal in Arizona. Even if all of your employees are licensed, I would not suggest paying anyone a flat fee based on closings.

In the past four years, the average price of the properties we've sold has dropped by *forty percent*, which has led to significantly lower commissions. Occasionally we sell very inexpensive properties and receive a commission check of $600 or less.

CHAPTER 7 –EMPOWERING EMPLOYEES

When your average commission is over $6,000 it might seem affordable to pay your Transaction Coordinator $200 per closing, but when your gross commission is $600, you would be paying *one-third* of your gross income to one employee!

How would you be able to pay the other members of your team? If your average commission drops like ours has, you will have to reduce the flat fee paid per transaction. The employee who was earning $200 per closing will resent the pay cut and will probably quit because of it!

Change in Real Life

<u>A Stake in the Outcome</u>

When you pay bonuses based on *income*, employees have no accountability for expenses. I once hired a new assistant and gave her a catalog to choose a headset. She chose an $800 Plantronics headset, the most expensive model in the catalog!

I reminded her that we share 20% of our profit with the employees in the department. I quickly calculated that $160 of the headset purchase would come from the employee bonus pool. I informed her that the other employees in the department would see the itemized list of expenditures and might not be very happy with her.

After our meeting, she opted to purchase the $300 version of the headset, which has worked reliably for the past two years.

In order to maximize your profit, you must teach your employees to think like a business owner.

SOLD ON CHANGE!

Do not set yourself up to lose a good employee over something you cannot control. Even before the home values fell, many markets were experiencing downward pressure on commissions.

Lower sale prices have resulted in lower real estate commissions all over the country. When you pay your employees a percentage of the profit, they will do everything they can to make the profit as large as possible. Be careful what you reward, because you will usually get it!

Empowering Your Staff

As Robert Kiyosaki says in his book, *Rich Dad, Poor Dad*, if your business cannot function without your constant intervention, you do not have a business; you have a *job!* A business functions whether you are there or not.

In order to convert your job into a *business*, you will have to remove yourself from all non-critical tasks. The definition of "critical" will vary among business owners and will change as your business grows.

It is easy to become so engrossed with the day-to-day tasks that you do not have any time to spend creating new business. Any time you find yourself so busy that you cannot take off at least one business day per week you should reassess the daily tasks that you perform and relinquish any that do not require your expertise. Take the time each week to review the results you are getting.

48

CHAPTER 7 –EMPOWERING EMPLOYEES

Small adjustments can produce hundreds of thousands in additional income over time just as small adjustments on a sailboat can alter the course by hundreds of miles. If you fail to modify your business in response to market changes, your business will suffer, stagnate, or die.

To determine which tasks to delegate and which tasks to keep, you will need to first list all of the tasks that you complete throughout the day (see discussion of TimeTracker™ on p. 37). You can then map your processes to create a flow chart so others can visualize the order in which things must occur. By grouping related tasks together, you can create separate specialized areas, or "departments," and delegate responsibility for those tasks to someone else.

Change in Real Life

"Hot Potato" Problem Solving

Failure to delegate decision-making ability to employees will severely limit the potential of any business. I witnessed this problem many times while working in large corporations.

If there was a problem on the manufacturing line, they passed it to the shift supervisor, who passed it to the line supervisor who passed it higher and higher up the chain of command.

When a decision was finally made by upper management and passed down to the employees on the line, they would scratch their head and ask, "Why are they doing *that*?" In my experience, decisions from "upper management" often attack the symptom, rather than the cause.

It is ludicrous to create a rigid structure where people who do not even understand the problem make the decisions on how to resolve it. I believe that the employees closest to problems are the best equipped to resolve them because they understand the issues better than anyone else. Employees will often devise a simple solution in a matter of minutes as they continue to do their job.

If you are a self-confessed "control freak" and will not delegate any decision-making to your employees, your business will never grow. To make time that will enable you to create more business, you must enable the employees and managers who work for you to make decisions within their departments.

Good employees are not *hired*; they are developed over time. You must give your employees the ability to grow and make mistakes or they will never learn. You can limit the severity of their mistakes by initially delegating only small decisions and then slowly expanding their decision-making authority as they become more experienced.

Employees make mistakes and so do you. Get used to it! When an employee makes the wrong decision, meet with them in private to understand what factors may have influenced them. Be sure to inform them up-front that they are not in any trouble and <u>never</u> scold or belittle them! If you do, they will never make another decision again and you will be forced to micro-manage your business forever.

CHAPTER 7 – EMPOWERING EMPLOYEES

Many times, there will be circumstances or underlying factors that you are not aware of, so it is crucial to get all of the information from your employees before you interject in the conversation. Take the time to listen and find out *why* they made the choice they did.

If after all the facts are presented, you do not agree with the employee's decision, calmly explain why you would have made a different choice and gently nudge them to see it your way. Use hypothetical situations to role-play with them to ensure that they understand and will make the correct decision the next time.

We enable every employee in our company to make decisions in their day-to-day tasks as long as the potential impact of their choice is less than $500. We have found that employees granted decision-making authority also develop a heightened sense of ownership for their job.

Giving your employees responsibility shows that you respect them. They will feel that you trust them and value their opinions. At first, they may be hesitant to make decisions and push the decision to you. Always push it back to them by asking, "What would you do?"

When employees make a decision to change a process, they must send an e-mail message to each department manager and the business owners to notify them of the change. This enables us to keep attuned to what is going on in our business without making all of the decisions ourselves.

SOLD ON CHANGE!

If an employee makes a change that we do not agree with, we meet with them to understand why they felt the change was necessary. Then we assess whether there may be any unforeseen consequences of the change.

8

Creating Culture

**Setting expectations that influence people's
behavior and define your company's image**

"No culture can live if it attempts to be exclusive."
– Mahatma Gandhi

SOLD ON CHANGE!

Starting a new company provides a blank slate on which to create an environment that will define your business. We named our company "Win3 Realty" to remind ourselves that each transaction should be a win for our clients, our company, and our community (win-win-win).

A win for the company means more than just the owners making a profit. The agents and the staff we employ need to benefit too. I personally review the paychecks every two weeks to ensure that the agents and staff are winning. Proactively addressing potential earnings problems enables us to catch them before it's too late.

Our company helps feed forty-five families in Tucson, so our largest expense by far is payroll. It takes a lot of time to recruit, hire, and train good employees. We do everything we can to compensate them fairly and make them feel valued so they will continue working with us. I believe that we enjoy low employee turnover because of our culture of caring about one another.

The best way a company can show that it cares for its employees is to offer them a good benefits package. Our full-time employees receive approximately half of their medical insurance, all of their dental insurance, eight paid holidays, and two weeks of paid vacation. We encourage our staff to become homeowners by crediting them *half* of the real estate commission we earn from selling a home to them (the Win3 agent who assisted them with the sale earns the other half of the commission).

CHAPTER 8 – CREATING CULTURE

We review company performance each week with the staff and celebrate major milestones with catered lunches, birthday celebrations, and occasional company outings. We allocate 20% of the company's profit toward bonuses to reward employees who have helped to make us successful.

When one member of our team falls behind on their work, other team members who are cross-trained in that department jump in to help. Nobody on our team wins unless we all win so everyone works hard and shares in the financial reward. If our employees need to earn extra income, we train them to set appointments for the agents or do work that we might otherwise contract out.

Peer pressure is our greatest stimulant. In a team environment, it is very difficult for one employee to slack off when all those around them are working tirelessly. To keep morale high, we have a "no negativity" policy in our company.

Our staff and agents are told when they are hired that they will receive <u>one</u> negativity warning in their *career*. This means NO back-biting, sniping, bad-mouthing, yelling, whining, complaining, or generally treating others with disrespect. We have had to enforce the policy only a few times with employees who thought they were irreplaceable, but turned out to be wrong!

We inform our clients of our "no negativity policy when we list their home, "If you're not happy with our service, you can cancel your listing with us. We'll tear up the contract and walk away, but our guarantee is double-sided..."

When they ask what that means I tell them, "If you call our office and start swearing at our staff or treating any of us with disrespect, we will be out the next day to get our sign. We take selling your home seriously and treat you and your sale with the utmost respect. We expect the same treatment in return. Life is just too short to work with angry people."

You'd be surprised how many clients tell me that they admire us for sticking up for our staff. No negativity applies to *everyone*. When you equip your employees to win, you have a much better chance of success. Employers who only care about themselves are destined to continually train new people because their best employees will leave them.

Change in Real Life

A Culture of Caring
Recently, the mother of an employee had a stroke and the employee needed time off work. The only problem was that she was out of vacation time.

Several of our employees volunteered to donate their paid vacation to this employee. Their generous gift is a perfect example of the team culture we've worked so hard to create.

The employees transferred their paid time off and our company matched each of their contributions. When faced with financial uncertainty, the employee received two weeks of paid time off to spend with her family. This culture of *caring* is not common at most companies! It makes me proud that we have it at our company.

CHAPTER 8 – CREATING CULTURE

Figure 8-1 Sales Record E-mail

From: Bob Zachmeier
Sent: Wednesday, September 16, 2009 3:08 AM
To: Win3 Realty Team; Win3 Agents
Subject: THANKS GUYS!!!

Win3 Team Members,

In case you haven't heard, we're catering in lunch for our entire team (agents and staff) tomorrow! Why? To celebrate the fact that today our team broke the all-time MLS sales record for the most transactions <u>ever</u> closed in Tucson in one calendar year! The cool thing is that we did it on September 15th with 107 days left in the year! Every day of the next 3-1/2 months we'll continue to push the bar higher than it's ever been before!

The previous sales record was set in 2005 by the designated broker of Lennar/US Homes during the best seller's market in Tucson history. That year their team sold a combined total of 335 homes at all of their site sales offices. Our team did it in less time, with <u>one</u> sales office, and only <u>ten</u> agents during the worst real estate market in decades!

Thanks to your efforts, I haven't personally closed a single transaction this year, nor have I set any appointments myself. For the first time ever, I'm spending 100% of my time working <u>on </u>our business rather than <u>in</u> it and the results show. Constantly implementing new ideas has helped us nearly double or triple our previous year's business during each of the past three years!

I'm excited because as well as we're doing, we still have less than a 2% market share which means there's still plenty of room for us to grow! Take pride in knowing that of the more than 700 real estate companies in Tucson, our small team is currently #7 in sales volume. Every company ahead of us has at least TEN TIMES the number of agents we have and nobody comes close to our productivity, which currently averages 33 sales per agent this year.

Thanks to all of you for helping us get here! It's been a fun ride to the top and we couldn't have done it without <u>YOU</u>!

Regards,

Bob Zachmeier
Broker/Owner - Win3 Realty
Tucson, AZ

Employee Benefits

It takes a lot of time to recruit and hire good employees. After hiring them, we spend months training them to become an expert at the tasks they perform each day.

After spending so much time and effort to find and train employees, it makes sense to protect our investment by trying to keep them working at our company. We offer our full-time staff members the following benefits:

- paid holidays
- paid time off from work
- employer-paid dental coverage
- employer-assisted medical insurance
- overtime when necessary to complete tasks
- flexible work schedule for family commitments
- performance bonus at major milestones
- housing assistance to purchase a home

Paid Holidays All employees receive eight paid holidays each year. Part-time employees receive four hours of holiday pay and full-time employees receive eight hours of pay on the following days: New Year's Day, Memorial Day, Independence Day, Labor Day, Thanksgiving Day, Black Friday (day after Thanksgiving), Christmas Day, Boxing Day (day after Christmas). If a holiday falls on a Saturday or Sunday, the next regular working day is the paid holiday.

Paid Time Off (PTO) is accrued by full-time employees after six months of employment. During the first five years of employment, PTO accrues at a rate of two weeks per year. For each successive year, an additional day of PTO accrues until an employee reaches a maximum of four weeks PTO per year.

Dental Coverage is available for full-time employees after six months of employment. The company pays the entire cost of Employers Dental Services (EDS) for eligible full-time employees. Part-time employees and employee's dependents may join the group policy at the employee's expense if allowed by the insurer.

Medical Insurance is available for eligible employees after six months of full-time employment. From time to time, the medical insurance provider and the amount paid by the company may change out of necessity. All eligible full-time employees receive the option to join the company's group coverage policy. Part-time employees and employee's dependents may join the group policy at the employee's expense if allowed by the insurer.

Overtime may be available to employees if they are unable to complete their tasks during their normal work schedule. All overtime requires approval in advance by a member of the management team. If approved for overtime, employees are limited to a maximum of 64 hours in any given week unless given prior written approval from a company owner or the office manager.

Flexible Work Schedules may be available to employees on a temporary basis to modify their scheduled shift to allow for doctor appointments, family needs, etc. A member of the management team will determine whether the time away will adversely affect the team or impact important deadlines. Management approves or denies the request based on company workload but the company strives to grant such requests whenever possible.

Home-Buyer Assistance enables employees to buy a home from one of our agents and receive half of the commission credited toward their closing costs, pre-paid expenses, and fees. The program is available for either personal residences or investment properties but is limited to one purchase per year. Win3 Realty also negotiates employee discounts on interest rates and loan fees with our lending partners. Employees and their spouses can also attend investment courses and first-time homebuyer seminars taught by the brokerage free of charge.

Company Performance Bonuses are available for all employees when the team achieves performance milestones. All team members are eligible to receive a quarterly bonus from Company profits when meeting certain profitability goals. Performance bonuses are directly proportional to company profits; the more the company earns, the more the employees earn.

9

Branches
of Business

**How to logically divide your company
into separate divisions and departments**

"Diversify your investments."– *John Templeton*

Branches of Business

Win3 Realty currently has five divisions that serve as pillars of our business. A diagram of our business structure is provided in Figure 9-1. We also have five departments that provide services and support for all divisions. Income and expenses for each division and department are isolated so we can establish the profitability of each.

Figure 9-1 Win3 Realty Business Structure

Win3 Realty Structure					
Admin. Dept.					
Advertising Dept.					
Offer Dept.	Residential Sales Division	Bank REO Division	Short Sale Division	Investor Division	Builder Division
Listing Dept.					
Transaction Dept.					

Residential Division - helps buyers find, negotiate, and purchase their dream home and assists sellers in marketing their property to attract the most interest. Within the Residential Division, we have an Inside Sales Department to contact leads and set appointments with prospective clients. The Outside Sales Department meets with prospective buyers and sellers to assist them in buying or selling property.

Bank REO Division - specializes in selling bank-owned properties for different banks and outsourcing companies. Banks refer to properties they have foreclosed on as Real Estate Owned (REO).

Short Sale Division - works with homeowners facing hardship who must sell their home for an amount less than what they owe to their bank or mortgage company.

Investor Division - assists real estate investors in meeting their investment goals by helping them analyze properties to determine whether they would be profitable as rentals or as "fix and flip" projects.

Builder Division – assists local builders in marketing their newly built homes and selling the homes of their clients who wish to buy a new home from the builder.

The Administration, Advertising, Listing, Offer, and Transaction Departments provide their services to each of the five divisions. A brief description of each Department is below. I have also included information about the REO, BPO, Repair, and Bookkeeping Departments within the REO Division.

A brief analysis of each department is provided below to indicate the personality type (see Chapter 4 – "Predicting Personality") of the employees we hire, the number of employees who currently work in that position, the number of properties that can be handled by each staff member, and the tasks that each department is responsible for completing.

Administrative Department

Personality Type: C/I
Current Employees: 1
Workload: One employee for every 500 listed properties

Tasks:

- Screen broker's calls to determine if another team member should handle
- Assist broker with answering e-mail and clerical tasks
- Make travel arrangements for conferences and meetings
- Set up broker's calendar and schedule appointments
- Assist broker in organization and filing of all information

Advertising Department

Personality Type: S/I
Current Employees: 1
Workload: One employee for every 500 listed properties

Tasks:

- Set up and maintain all websites with current information
- Order signs, sign riders, and ad space
- Design flyers and sales campaigns to attract clients
- Coordinate open houses and caravan tours
- Monitor automated lead generation tools and track results
- Calculate expenses and results to determine cost for each lead type
- Coordinate training events and recruiting seminars

CHAPTER 9 – BRANCHES OF BUSINESS

Offer Department
> Personality Type: S/I
> Current Employees: 2
> Workload: One employee for every 175 offers per month

Tasks:
- Answer office phones and route calls to appropriate department
- Answer questions and assist selling agents
- Possess the patience of a saint
- Upload and track offers in the online database
- Verify completeness and accuracy of offers and loan pre-qualification letters
- Notify buyers, sellers, agents, and the title company of the acceptance/rejection/expiration of offers on listed properties

Listing Department
> Personality Type: C
> Current Employees: 2
> Workload: One employee for every 175 listed properties

Tasks:
- MLS data input
- Activation and cancellation of utilities on REO properties
- Obtain feedback from property showings and provide to clients
- Verify HOA name, contact information and monthly fee
- Create list of properties to be visited and tasks to be completed each day

Transaction Department
Personality Type: C
Current Employees: 3
Workload: One employee for every 50 transactions/month

Tasks:
- Communicate every three days with Buyer's agent, Buyer's lender, and title company
- Coordinate inspections
- Notify Repair Department of repair requests for company listings
- Keep Buyer's lender on track with constant reminders
- When Buyer's lender doesn't perform, call them on it
- Generate a "cure" notice and provide to both listing and selling agent when contract terms are not adhered to
- Collect all transaction paperwork and ensure accuracy
- Submit everything to title & schedule closing
- Push, push, push!

REO Department
Personality Type: C
Current Employees: 4
Workload: One employee for every 75 assigned properties

Tasks:
- Monitor all client portals to ensure tasks are not late
- Accept new REO property assignments
- Issue alert to all departments to add new properties
- Provide occupancy information to Asset Manager
- Distribute e-mails to department where they need to go

REO Department (continued)
- Play "Whack-A-Mole" by allocating 600 daily e-mail tasks from REO clients to the department responsible
- Refer all communication about property/market status to broker
- Coordinate contractor quotes and repairs with Repair Department
- Rank offers in order of the highest net to the bank and submit on client portal
- Upload documents to Asset Managers
- Forward all Broker Price Opinion (BPO) and /Monthly Status Report (MSR) requests to BPO Department

BPO Department
Personality Type: C
Current Employees: 7
Workload: 10 BPOs per agent per day

Tasks:
- Enter BPO request into BPO Genius
- Track due dates, issue photo requests
- Pull comps/input generic MLS data
- Review accuracy of data input and validity of comps
- Input market information & review comp prices (gut check)
- Verify that required photos are taken, notices were posted, worksheet is complete with neighborhood factors and repairs noted, key safes, contractor boxes, & sign riders were installed, and marketing materials were left at properties

Repair Department
Personality Type: C
Current Employees: 3
Workload: One employee for every 50 properties

Tasks:
- Obtain list of required repairs from BPO Department
- Order contractor quotes for all required repairs noted on list
- Forward contractor quotes to REO Department for upload to client portals
- Order repairs when approved by clients
- Meet contractors at properties to ensure work was done satisfactorily
- Verify that we have both "before" and "after" photos

Bookkeeping Department
Personality Type: C
Current Employees: 2
Workload: One employee for every 150 assigned properties

Tasks:
- Trusted person to write checks and enter all expenses in QuickBooks
- Have owner review and sign all checks before mailing
- Submit weekly report to owners showing monies owed
- Collect time cards and pay employees
- Oversee Accounting staff
- Upload of bills and checks to REO clients and track accounts by client to determine unpaid balances

10

Knowing
Your Numbers

**What to track in each department to ensure
that your initial assumptions are still accurate**

*"It is important that you recognize your progress and take
pride in your accomplishments."– Rosemarie Rossetti*

SOLD ON CHANGE!

In order to set goals to change your business, you must first determine where your business is now. Then you have to decide where you want it to go and the actions it will take to get it there.

Your business will be most profitable when you are in control of your numbers. You need to know what is working and what isn't, which vendors are paying and which aren't, where your advertising works and where it doesn't, where your business comes from and where it doesn't, who's setting appointments and who isn't, who's writing offers and who isn't, and who's closing deals and who isn't.

As mentioned earlier, we track the income and expenses separately for each division in our company. If more than one division occupies a building, we split the overhead costs using the percentage of the space each division occupies so we can ascertain the profitability of each division.

Every week at staff meetings, each department is responsible for providing key metrics. For each measurable item, we use a simple spreadsheet to show the goal we expected, the actual number received, and the actual numbers from the previous three weeks. This helps us quickly spot market shifts that will affect our income and expenses.

This information enables us to quickly compare the results expected with the results received during the previous four weeks so we can determine whether a new trend is developing.

CHAPTER 10 – KNOWING YOUR NUMBERS

By proactively tracking our business, we can forecast our pending workload and make assessments of which departments are likely to become overwhelmed in the coming weeks.

Rather than waiting until the workload increases, we try to have people hired and trained before there is a need. For instance, we know that an increase in listing activity will increase the number of sign calls. The sign calls will increase the number of agents we need available for appointments.

More agents handling more appointments will create more offers, which will ultimately lead to more transactions. We know that our transaction team members can each handle about 50 open escrows at a time, so if we detect an increase in offer activity we can hire a new employee and have them in training for three weeks before the transaction workload increases.

We know how much each form of advertising costs to create and maintain and the advertising campaign that caused each client to contact us. This information allows us to calculate the exact cost of each new contact and the effectiveness of each advertising campaign. By doing more of what works and less of what does not work, we continually improve our results!

By tracking the number of leads that come in and appointments distributed to each agent, we can calculate the conversion rate of leads to appointments for each Inside Sales Associate and the closing rate of each Outside Sales agent.

If you have one agent who closes 80% of their appointments and another who closes only 30%; who would you give the most promising appointments to?

If you guessed the 30% agent, you are wrong! Even if a Seller called and said they were sitting at their kitchen table with a pen in their hand waiting to sign a listing agreement, we would send the agent with the 80% conversion rate because the agent who converts only 30% of their appointments has a 70% chance of screwing it up!

We meet one-on-one with those who produce unacceptable conversion rates to determine why they are struggling. The meeting usually results in retraining, relocation, or removal.

Below are the items we track in each area of our business:

Residential Sales Division

Inside Sales - tracks the date and time each lead is received, the number of leads assigned to each agent, the number of calls attempted and whether it was the 1st, 2nd, or 3rd attempt, the number of successful contacts, the percentage of new leads called back, the number of appointments set for each agent, the number of appointments actually held, the percentage of appointments set from all calls, the time spent on calls, the number of leads added to the incubation campaign, and the number of incubation calls made to the clients in waiting.

Outside Sales - tracks the number of appointments scheduled, appointments that were actually held, the percentage of clients who showed up for their appointment, the number of appointments with incomplete outcome, the number of Buyer/Broker agreements signed, the number of listing agreements signed, the number of offers submitted, the number of offers accepted, and the number of transactions closed on both Win3 leads and personal sphere leads.

Bank REO Division
REO Department - tracks the number of documents to upload, the number of documents due for submission on each client portal, the number of offers to upload, the number of tasks on each portal that are coded yellow or red (due or overdue), the number of tasks that are more than one day old, the number of occupancy checks completed, the number of cash-for-key negotiations conducted, and the number of tasks escalated for resolution.

Repair Department (REO) - tracks the number of contractor bids outstanding, the bid packages submitted, the total number of projects completed, the number of yards initially cleaned, the number of yards maintained, the number of properties trashed out and initially cleaned, the number of invoices submitted to bookkeeping, and the number of properties in some state of repair.

Bookkeeping Department - tracks the total number of invoices to submit to REO clients, the number of invoices submitted, the number of rejected invoice reimbursements, the number of reimbursements submitted for broker assistance, the number of properties with outstanding reimbursements, and the amount of the outstanding reimbursements by bank and by property.

Short Sale Division - tracks the total number of marketing pieces sent, the quantity of each marketing piece, the number of agent e-mails responded to, the number of lead calls received, the number of appointments set, the percentage of appointments set, the number of appointments held, the number of new clients secured, the amount of fees collected, the number of short sales in offer status, the number under contract, and the number closed each month.

Service Departments
Advertising Department - tracks the total number of leads received from each type of advertising and from each advertising campaign. For each division we track the total leads received, the percentage of the overall total, the number of appointments set, the percentage of appointments from each source, and the cost for each type of lead.

Offer Department - tracks the number of offers received each week, the number uploaded into the online database, the number that were accepted, the number that were rejected, the number of offers that were made on our listed properties, the number of offers that were made on properties listed with other brokers, and the total number of offers handled in the month.

Listing Department - tracks the number of active, active contingent, pending, and sold properties, the number that are in pre-market and not yet listed, those expiring, the number newly assigned, and the number of properties listed for 30 days with no offers or showing activity.

Transaction Department - tracks the properties under contract, the number of new transactions each week, the number of closed transactions for the month, the number of transactions loaded into the online database, those that are missing paperwork, the number with potential issues that are due to close, and the number of transactions handled by each employee.

11

Duties to Delegate

How to organize your life, map your work flow, and delegate tasks to your employees

"You must be on top of change or change will be on top of you"
– Mark Victor Hansen

The fastest way to accomplish something is to find someone who has already done it. Study them, learn from their mistakes, and shamelessly copy what they have done. Our business, Win3 Realty, could not have grown by 1,000% in three years without help and a *plan*.

As I mentioned earlier, coaching has provided many innovative ideas that have helped us sell more homes than we had ever dreamed possible. Since getting a coach in 2005, I have not missed a single opportunity to attend a conference. You might think that fifteen straight conferences with the same coach would become repetitive, but I continue to learn and grow with each conference I attend.

At a recent SuperConference, Craig Proctor interviewed Gary Keller; co-founder of Keller-Williams Realty Inc. Gary informed the audience that he has utilized several coaches throughout his life and that he is still being coached even though he owns one of the most successful real estate franchises in the world. I have provided a top ten list of Gary Keller's success strategies below:

1) The three secrets to success are blocking your time to have a specific start and end for each task, creating written Action Plans of what you need to accomplish, and developing repeatable Scripts & Dialogs to use in getting your point across.

2) Don't let your *willpower* determine your success.

3) Always ask yourself, "Who is going to be my next coach?" You will always work harder for a coach than you will for yourself.

4) Write down ten things you are doing to attract business. Select the three that work the best and throw away the other seven. Then add one new thing that works.

5) Be more focused, accountable, and *expect* better results.

6) Time does not matter; how you *use* your time matters. Trading time for money doesn't work, so double your production and halve your time!

7) Napoleon Hill, author of *Think and Grow Rich*, found that the reason most people fail is they stop too soon and they don't associate with the right people. Half of success is what you *do*, the other half *who you do it with*.

8) Do more; talk less. At the end of each day be able to say, "I'm glad I did" instead of "I wish I had."

9) Don't live a life of regret. Ask yourself, "What more could my life be?" If you're doing all that you *can* do, ask yourself whether you're doing all that *could* be done. Your habits might be holding you back!

10) If you are at the edge of life's container, find out how to get a bigger container. How *big* can you imagine your life? God can imagine it pretty big so why are *you* screwing it up?

Organizing and Mapping Your Workflow

Planning your life and your business is an important step that many people skip. If you or any of your employees cannot be replaced, you have a problem. Everyone, including you, needs be able to take time off from work to re-energize. If nobody knows how to do the work when you or key employees are away, your business will suffer. Take the time to develop a job description for each task and make a flow chart for your company that starts with advertising for new business and ends with client follow-up after closing.

After you and all of your employees have completed the TimeTracker™ exercise for several days, copy the tasks for each team member into a separate column of an Excel worksheet. Arrange the tasks in each employee's column in the order they would occur throughout the sales process.

The completed sheet should have each employee in a separate column and the tasks in each column sorted by the order they occur, with the first task at the top of the sheet and the last task at the bottom of the sheet.

Look across every employee's column and find the task that occurs first, second, third, etc. Draw an arrow from the first task to the second task with the arrow ending at the second task. Draw another arrow from the second task to the third task with the arrow ending on the third task. Continue this exercise for all of the tasks done by all employees.

If your arrows are repeatedly going back and forth between staff members, you should reallocate the work into departments to form a smoother process flow so employees are not constantly pushing work back and forth between them. Reallocate the tasks so there are few, if any, back and forth transfers and define each task as follows:

- Required input to complete task: _____

- Input provided by: _____ Department

- Required output to complete task: _____

- Output provided to: _____ Department

If you ask your employees who their customer is, most will refer to the clients who are buying or selling their home. We educate our employees that their customer is the person who receives the output of their work. In most cases, the employee's "customer" is their co-worker.

Defining the input needed for an employee to complete their job also defines the output required for the previous job. Each employee's performance is measured by how well they equip the next employee to do their job.

This analysis will take some time to complete, but should be done for each task by the person who typically completes the task. When the employee thinks they have captured all aspects of the task, take their written procedure and try to complete the task using only their instructions. There are usually gaps in the process because portions of the job are so ingrained in the employee's routine and they do not even think about doing them any more.

When you can perform each of the employee's tasks from start to finish by following the systematic written instructions, you will have a repeatable process. The written instructions will enable you to train new employees and cross-train other staff members in a much shorter time. Completing this process for tasks in each department will result in an operations manual for your business.

The easy-to-follow instructions will enable you to add personnel or reassign tasks easily as your volume increases or decreases. Cross-trained employees can easily shift jobs during peaks and valleys in the business cycle to help out in the departments stressed with unusual volume.

Many bank clients require the real estate agents who work for them to create a written disaster recovery plan. Most people immediately think of offsite data storage and replacement of computer equipment, but if your company does not have documented task descriptions, a disaster is waiting to happen! What if a key employee is injured or killed? Written processes for each repeatable task in your business should be part of your disaster recovery plan.

12

Take Time to Transition

How to reallocate your time to become proactive rather than reactive

"Life is like a coin. You can spend it any way you wish, but you only spend it once."– Lillian Dickson

SOLD ON CHANGE!

Everyone, no matter how rich or poor, has only 24 hours per day. How you utilize time determines how wealthy you are, how often you see your family, how much you exercise, etc. In essence, how you spend your time determines what you accomplish in life.

As new events occur in our lives, we modify our schedules to accommodate them. Before you can make changes in your life, you must allot time in your schedule for the new action to occur. You cannot be at client appointments and school plays at the same time so you prioritize them and skip, cancel, or reschedule appointments of lower importance.

How do you determine which tasks to delegate and which to keep doing yourself? The best method I have found is to keep a log of how I spend my time each day. I use a simple Microsoft Excel spreadsheet that divides each hour into ten six-minute increments. As I complete tasks throughout the day, I simply write how long the task took into the appropriate space on my TimeTracker™ spreadsheet. This productivity tool will assist in documenting how you spend your time each day. An electronic copy is available free of charge on my website at: www.soldonchange.com.

After logging the way you spend your time for two to five days, you will be surprised to find how much time you spend on situations in which your efforts cannot change the outcome. Review each task on the TimeTracker™ sheet to determine whether your expertise was necessary.

If your decision-making ability was not required, estimate the amount of money you would have to pay someone to complete all of the tasks that do not require your expertise.

To make time available to take on new activities, you will need to delegate to staff members all of the tasks that do not require your knowledge, skill, or ability. Be sure to include all of the tasks that you dislike because you will probably put them off anyway or not address them at all.

If you find yourself doing menial tasks after your employees have all gone home for the day, you need to delegate better! You should delegate all tasks that someone else can complete inexpensively. This includes personal errands.

After you have removed yourself from all non-critical activities, be careful not to fill the newly-found time with other non-critical activities. Before becoming involved in any situation, ask this question, "Will my involvement change the outcome?" If you cannot change it, then <u>delegate</u> it!

Repeat this exercise at least four times per year to maximize your effectiveness. Tasks that were critical several months earlier may not retain their same importance as your business grows. At some point, you will need to delegate tasks that require highly skilled personnel hired specifically for that task. As long as the time you save is used to earn more than you pay an employee, the cost will be worth it. You need to focus your efforts on doing what you are best at.

SOLD ON CHANGE!

Your employees should complete this exercise too, especially when they tell you they need help because they do not have enough time to do their job. When this happens, I have often found that they are spending too much effort on time-consuming tasks that produce no value.

Change in Real Life

A TimeTracker™ Surprise

After a recent TimeTracker™ exercise, I found that members of our administrative staff were spending several hours each week to create driving maps so our agents could find their way to listing appointments!

Before hiring additional employees, ask your current staff to run the TimeTracker exercise to find out how they are *really* spending their time. You may not need more people, just more <u>focus</u>.

Reactionary Agents

When people with Sales jobs wake up each morning, they never know whether they will have any income that day. When their phone rings, they spring into action, cancelling whatever they had planned to scurry across town on short notice to meet with a prospect.

Calls from potential clients occur so sporadically that many agents feel the need to sacrifice their time with family and friends because they don't know when the next opportunity will come.

CHAPTER 12 – TAKE TIME TO TRANSITION

I know this is true because I *was* that agent who dropped everything to meet a client's needs. I allowed real estate to control my life and take priority over my wife for five years! When a potential client would call, I'd stop whatever I was doing to pick up the phone and then race out the door a few minutes later.

I cannot count the number of times I ate cold dinners, missed movie endings, and rescheduled or cancelled weekend plans in order to please a potential client. Many real estate agents let this go on too long and end up getting divorced. Thankfully, I am blessed with an understanding spouse who persevered during those years.

We got our lives back on track by running our business *proactively* rather than reactively. We changed the way we advertised, used technology to capture clients, and developed systems to work more effectively. Our perception of scarcity was replaced by an assurance of *plenty* when we began to generate more prospects than we could handle.

Most prospects who call about a home expect you to drop whatever you happen to be doing, drive across town, and show them the home immediately. However, not everyone who calls is ready or able to buy. A simple script from Craig Proctor with non-threatening questions helps us determine whether each caller's timing and motivation are right. We use the script to find out exactly where potential buyers are in the home buying process.

We've learned how to give our clients what they want without disrupting our lives to do it. The secret is to offer something that your competitors don't have to offer. If the prospect perceives value in your proposition, they'll be willing to schedule the meeting at a time when you're available. But you must provide a *reason* for them to come to you.

For us that's easy because we provide market data that other companies don't. The data we use is available to every member of our local real estate board but most agents don't spend the time and effort to collect and chart the data in a meaningful way.

Do you think potential buyers might like to know whether homes in the neighborhoods they're considering are increasing or decreasing in value? Of course they would! We ask them, "Don't you think it's worth twenty minutes of your time to find out which areas are increasing in value and which are still in decline? What time is better for you to come to our office, Tuesday afternoon or Wednesday morning?"

After establishing a time and place to meet, ensure that you have the correct spelling of the caller's name, their work, home, and cell phone numbers, and their e-mail address. Before ending the call, repeat the agreed upon time to meet and be sure to remind them *why* they're coming to your office by saying, "we look forward to seeing you on Friday to show you the fastest appreciating neighborhoods in your price range." Reiterating the reason for the meeting will significantly reduce the number of "no show" appointments you experience.

CHAPTER 12 – TAKE TIME TO TRANSITION

When we meet prospective clients at our office, every Buyer and Seller is given a brief market presentation so they will understand the supply and demand for homes in the area where they want to buy or sell. We educate our clients about seasonal trends and point out where we currently are in the cycle.

Most people with families prefer to move when their kids are out of school so in the Tucson market there are usually twice as many buyers in the summer as there are in the winter. We educate our sellers of this fact and explain that since May, June, and July are the best months to sell, they cannot afford to have their home overpriced during the summer selling season.

We educate our buyers that the between Thanksgiving and Christmas very few families are actively seeking a home. The holiday season is usually the best time to buy because the last thing on anyone's mind is taking down the holiday decorations so that they can move during the most stressful time of the year. If the buyers don't want to wait until December, we educate them so they'll be able to write better offers to beat other buyers.

Educating your clients takes more time upfront, but they will have a better chance at success with the information you provide. In my experience, clients who haven't been educated about the market have a lower likelihood of having their contract accepted and a higher likelihood of falling out during the transaction.

SOLD ON CHANGE!

Your willingness and ability to educate your clients will set you apart from other real estate agents. If your clients feel that you understand the market, they'll seek you out for advice before making a decision to buy or sell.

13

Probing Your Prospects

How to determine the motivation and timing of prospects before you meet with them

"If after observation and analysis, you find that anything agrees with reason and is conducive to the good and benefit of one and all, then accept it."– Buddha

SOLD ON CHANGE!

Real estate prospects can usually be divided into three major groups. The groups and the percentage of distribution are provided below:

1) 10% will never buy or sell (at least not from you).
2) 10% might buy or sell from you and are ready *now.*
3) 80% might buy or sell from you but are not ready now.

The 10% in the first group who will never buy or sell from you could be nosey neighbors, financially unqualified, or might have a close friend or relative who is a real estate agent. It's important to identify this group quickly so you don't spend much time on them.

The best indicator I've found to establish a prospect's intent is to insist on meeting at our office before showing them any homes. If you have ever driven an hour across town to show a home only to find that the prospect's grandfather is a real estate agent, you will appreciate why we do this. It will significantly reduce amount of time and gasoline you waste on such endeavors. Besides saving time, this step is necessary to educate your clients about the price range and demand in the neighborhood where they are considering a purchase.

The 10% in the second group who are ready to buy or sell now could turn out to be a much higher percentage depending on where the inquiry originated. Usually the buyers who are driving around calling on signs are much further along in the home-buying process than those conducting internet searches. During times when we've had more than 300 properties listed, the percentage of people who fell into this group has been much higher than 10%.

That leaves 80% in the third group who will buy or sell at some point, just not now. Many agents who encounter this group of prospective clients intend to follow up with them when the time is right, but it seldom happens. According to the National Association of REALTORS®, the average real estate agent sells only two homes per year. Many agents with few sales focus on the *now* buyers and sellers because they don't have a steady stream of closings and need to pay their bills.

Because the number of potential clients who are not yet ready to act is eight times greater than those who are ready to act now, it's crucial to create a system to proactively capture and incubate these clients until they're ready. We use a series of e-mails and phone calls to stay in contact with the people in this category and track them in our SalesJunction database (see Chapter 25 – "Capturing Clients").

During the first six months of 2009, more than 4,000 prospects contacted our office. We distributed the leads to nine sales agents for follow up. If at least 10% of those contacts were ready to act, we should have had 400 opportunities to make a sale. Our best agents convert 80% or more of the clients they meet with so it seems logical that we could convert at least 50% on average. If that were the case, we would have closed 200 sales during the first half of the year. But we only closed 45 sales, which represents only 1.1% of the total prospects.

Through a series of "autopsy calls" to buyers and sellers who didn't use our company, we determined that most individuals had either never been contacted by the agent we assigned to them or they were disqualified by the agent because they weren't immediately ready to act. By giving each agent an average of 74 leads per month we'd inadvertently sent a message that it was okay to drop as many as they wanted because there would be plenty more the next day.

It was then that I realized that most agents don't think like business owners. Many have no desire to earn a lot of money; they are in the business because it is easier than punching a time clock. They sell until they've earned enough to pay their bills and then they stop.

If I sell three homes during the first week of the month, I think, "Wow, this is going to be a *great* month!" In the same situation many of the agents I've hired (and fired) over the years would think, "Great! Now I don't have to work for the rest of the *year!*"

I've found that an agent who sells two homes per year will sell two homes per year no matter if you give them two leads or two hundred leads. We spent a lot of time and money to advertise, answer the phone, glean information, enter it into our tracking system, and assign the lead to the agent. When I discovered that the leads were not being properly handled, I took them away from the agents.

Real estate agents are independent contractors who you cannot tell when or how hard to work. We started an Inside

Sales Department with employees who we could tell *what* to do, *how* to do it, and *when* to do it. We now screen the calls, incubate the prospects that aren't yet ready to act, and book appointments with those who are.

With our Inside Sales staff in place, during the same six-month period in 2010 we received roughly the same number of client contacts as we did in 2009, but closed three times more transactions than when the sales agents were making the calls.

We're continually improving our conversion process to provide quality appointments to our ever-increasing team of sales agents. A steady stream of qualified appointments will help retain good sales agents because they will earn a lot more money working within our system than they could on their own.

This system is set up to feed on itself. The monthly brokerage fees that we collect from our sales agents pay the wages of the support staff hired to set appointments. The more appointments we produce, the more agents we attract and thus the more fees we collect. More fees pay more support staff to produce more leads and set more appointments.

Inside Sales is the most important component of our Residential real estate division. In fact, the conversion of leads to qualified appointments affects the success of every department in our company because their success depends on the number of prospects converted to clients at the initial point of contact.

SOLD ON CHANGE!

Successful call conversion can mean the difference between being very profitable and losing money. One lost opportunity each week may not seem like a lot, especially when you receive hundreds or thousands of calls each year, but it can make a tremendous difference in your *profit*.

If you lose one call per week that could have been converted to an appointment, you lose the opportunity to meet with *fifty-two* potential clients each year. If on average, you convert 80% of the prospects you meet to clients, you will have forty-one fewer Buyer/Broker agreements signed each year. If 90% of those who sign a Buyer/Broker with you generate an offer, you will write thirty-seven fewer offers. If 80% of the offers you write are accepted and close, you will have lost the commission generated by 30 home sales each year.

Failing to return <u>one</u> call per week could cost you *ten times more* than the average agent earns all year! If your average commission check is $5,000, you could earn $150,000 more per year if you just convert that *one* extra appointment each week!

Appointment setting is so important it should be the very last thing that you delegate to someone else on your team!

14

Converting Clients

Why and how we use employees, not agents to convert lead calls to appointments

"I'm slowly becoming a convert to the principle that you can't motivate people to do things, you can only de-motivate them."
– Dilbert

SOLD ON CHANGE!

Salespeople often skip the important step of creating a *need* for the client to use them. Many real estate agents rely on the fact that buyers need someone with an electronic key to open a home, but <u>all</u> agents have an electronic key. You must create a reason for clients to use YOU or they won't be *your* clients for long.

Most people will walk into an auto parts store and go straight to the counter to ask for help, but at a car dealership or a shoe store they will repel the advancing salesperson by generating an unrehearsed response of, "I'm just looking." Even professional salespeople do this. I finally understand why.

In an auto parts store many of the items are stored in racks behind the counter and you need assistance from the store personnel to find what you're looking for. In contrast, at a shoe store or car dealership, all of the products are on display and it's very easy to walk up and down the aisles to view the different styles without any assistance. If the salesperson who approaches doesn't present a benefit, we'll repel them because we don't feel that we *need* them.

What if you walked into a shoe store and were met at the door by someone who said, "Welcome to Shoe World, is this your first visit with us or are you a returning customer?" Most people would answer this question because it is inoffensive and doesn't commit them to buying anything from the salesperson.

No matter whether they say that they are a returning customer or a new customer, the salesperson would say, "Well, for our _____ customers, today we're offering 10% off on all of the shoes on these five racks. I'll leave you alone to take a look around, but if you have any questions or can't find your size, my name is Jerry and I'll be right over there to assist you if you need help."

I don't know about you, but I would no longer have the desire to repel Jerry with the "I'm just looking" line. Why? Because by offering a benefit, Jerry created a need for me to use him. If you found a pair of shoes that you liked, would you attempt to locate Jerry? Of course you would! I'd track him down even if he was in the break room to get my discount!

Change in Real Life

__Track Your Leads__

Anyone who has visited our office can attest to the fact that our staff squeezes the life out of every lead. They chase agents to find out what happened to each call and perform "autopsy calls" to find out why the lead didn't choose the agent we sent to their home. My friend Steve Cruz visited our office with two staff members. He and his staff were so impressed by our system for tracking leads that he hired two of our staff members to set up our system at his office in San Antonio, TX.

Inside Sales Pay Plan Details

We find and hire most of our staff members by placing online ads on www.craigslist.com under the Sales Jobs, Real Estate jobs, and Part-time categories. An example of an ad we might use is provided below in Figure 14-1.

Figure 14-1 Craigslist Inside Sales Ad

> # HELP!
> Busy North side real estate office
> needs help booking appointments!
> **Never any "Cold Calling!"**
> We have more calls than we can return!
> Work SMARTER, not HARDER!
>
> Staff members who follow our
> script earn over $40.00 per hour!
> For a phone interview, e-mail your
> resume and cover letter to:
> XXXXXXX@XXX.com
> Real estate license not required
> Be sure to Reference ad #5F639

When reviewing applicants' resumes we look for a solid employment history without a lot of jumping around. Sales experience is not necessary if the script is followed, but employees with previous sales positions at auto parts stores, clothing stores, or similar places have worked out well for us because they have all learned to follow a script.

CHAPTER 14 – CONVERTING CLIENTS

I believe that inside sales should be a part-time position with time slots of no more than two or three consecutive hours. People can physically work longer than that but we've found that their conversion declines sharply after a few hours of making calls.

Employees working long shifts are far less successful at conversion at the end of their shift than they were at the beginning of the shift. It takes time and money to attract prospective clients. Allowing burned-out employees to buzz through leads without booking any appointments is a huge waste of your advertising investment!

We start new employees at minimum wage for the first two weeks while they learn and practice the script. After another two weeks we can usually determine whether the employee will be a good fit for our company. A career in phone sales is not for everyone. We typically hire the top three or four candidates we interview and train them all at the same time. It would be great if all of them would work out but usually two or three quit within a few weeks.

Most of the Inside Sales Associates (ISAs) on our team are <u>not</u> licensed. In Arizona, setting an appointment does not require a real estate license. Some of our employees have past sales experience and others have none. We've found that unlicensed people are more reliable, follow the script better, and get better results than licensed individuals.

Below, are some of the problems we've experienced with giving leads directly to our agents:

- They tend to "cherry pick" the leads that they feel will result in the fastest sale and ignore the rest

- When they get busy with clients, they don't return lead calls

- They attempt to sell over the telephone before having outlined the benefits of using our company.

Unlicensed staff members don't get busy with clients and can't talk about price. They follow the script because they are not paid unless the caller attends the appointment and is qualified to buy. Inside Sales Associates don't like their pay to be tied to how good or bad the Outside Sales agents are at converting and closing the prospects. We pay our ISA staff a base pay of $10.00 per hour so we can tell them when to come and who to call.

In addition to their base pay, they receive a $20.00 flat fee for every qualified and motivated prospect that comes to the office for an appointment with an agent on our team. Non-licensed employees cannot be compensated based on the *outcome* of a sale but they <u>can</u> be compensated when a qualified prospect shows up at appointments.

Two of our ISAs are full-time employees who work in other positions at our company. In their spare time after work, these women consistently earn more than $40.00 per hour setting appointments. I like this arrangement because it gives our employees the opportunity to earn extra money and makes it less likely that they will find a better paying job somewhere else and leave. We also avoid the overhead associated with hiring additional employees because the benefits of the existing employees have already been paid.

If an ISA sets two good appointments in one hour, they receive $20.00 for each appointment set plus their $10.00 per hour wage. Although $50.00 per hour may sound like a lot, I'd be thrilled if every ISA earned at least that much or more because we have no way to recover the $10.00 paid to an ISA who works one hour and sets no appointments. The employee who set two qualified appointments gave us two opportunities to sell a home and potentially earn thousands of dollars on each sale.

If only one appointment is set per hour, the average cost per appointment is $30.00 ($20.00 for setting the appointment and $10.00 in hourly wage). However, if two appointments are set per hour, our cost is reduced to $25.00 per lead ($20.00 for setting the appointment and *half* of their $10.00 per hour wage).

Paying $25 or $30 per prospective client may seem expensive, but it's common in the industry to pay a referral fee of 25 or 30 *percent* of the gross commission for only a name and a phone number. The prospects scheduled for appointments drive across town to meet with us at our office and are usually more motivated than those we meet at a property.

If a potential client doesn't show up for their appointment, is not qualified to purchase a home, or is not ready to buy or sell, the Inside Sales employee receives only their hourly pay. Our pay structure motivates the ISA staff to book appointments with only *qualified* candidates!

Asking the clients to answer a few questions and to drive to our office usually does a good job of screening out the tire-kickers, nosey neighbors, and *mean* people.

Clients who are rude on the initial call tend to get even nastier during the buying or selling process. They can sap your energy with their sarcastic remarks and blatant rudeness. We prefer not to subject either our staff or agents to this type of behavior.

When we switched to this pay plan in March 2010, the Outside Sales Agents (OSAs) reported a dramatic improvement in both the ability and motivation of the prospects they met with. Some OSAs even said the appointments were the best we had ever set for them! Within three months of hiring the ISA team, our fourteen OSAs had 66 concurrent residential closings in escrow, an all-time high!

15

Commission Considerations

Determining which services to provide agents and how to split the commission

"I cannot give you the formula for success, but I can give you the formula for failure: which is: Try to please everybody."
– Herbert B. Swopettee

SOLD ON CHANGE!

Any successful real estate brokerage has either a large number of agents paying a small monthly fee or a small number of agents paying a large monthly fee. I have observed that 5% of real estate agents make 95% of the money, so I don't want to employ the *most* agents; I want to employ the *most productive* agents. To help our agents become more productive, we have taken most non-selling tasks away from them. We do the marketing, answer the calls, and set appointments for them.

In Arizona, many of the large brick and mortar real estate offices are shutting down. The country club office model is dying because of lower commissions. Agents who desire a large prestigious office are having a harder time finding brokerages that offer such trappings. Due to computers, scanners, and cellular telephones, more agents are working remotely from inexpensive virtual offices in their homes.

We do not assign desks to our agents, in fact we ask them to leave the sales office when they are not meeting with clients. We have desks available for client appointments but don't encourage agents to stay in the office all day. Many agents are very talkative and can become "time vampires" if you let them. Their desire to chat with your staff can adversely affect productivity. We moved the agents out of our main office for this reason.

Our ISA staff is available to help the agents during core hours but during the best times to contact clients, they lock their office door and hang a "Do Not Disturb" sign similar to the red "on the air" lights at a radio station.

CHAPTER 15 – COMMISSION CONSIDERATIONS

To reduce the number of interruptions from agents, our staff gently reminds the agents that one of the biggest reasons they came to our company is because we provide them with motivated clients, "In order for us to set appointments for you, we need to be able to return calls quickly!"

We could charge each agent for the number of leads they receive but that penalizes top producers who meet with dozens of clients and rewards slackers who meet with only a few clients. A flat fee provides an incentive for *everyone* to sell. The more homes the agents sell, the cheaper their fee per sale becomes!

Agents who hustle can make a lot of money selling homes but as discussed earlier, many real estate agents sell just enough homes to pay their bills. With a limitless supply of leads, an unmotivated agent will become like a fussy cat that sniffs at food and then walks away. When asked what happened to the leads you gave them, these agents will tell you that the prospect is not qualified or that the lead quality is poor. The truth is that they either disqualified the lead or never followed up.

We run a business, not a social program. Although we strive to provide two appointments per week per agent, we make no commitment to assign appointments evenly or guarantee that the agents will each receive a certain number of clients. We made that mistake once and learned a painful lesson.

We assign appointments to the agents who tell us what happened to their last appointment. If several agents are available during the time a client has requested, we choose the agent with the skill set and personality that best matches the client's needs.

If the agents don't convert their appointments using our presentations or we don't get feedback on what happened to their last prospect, they won't receive new appointments. This competitive system keeps agents motivated because they *want* appointments and know that if they don't follow through, they won't receive any more.

We also encourage our agents to find business on their own rather than becoming dependent on us finding clients for them. We provide tools to help our agents generate referral business and we encourage them financially by compensating their sphere referrals with a higher commission split than we pay on company-generated transactions. The goal is to turn each company transaction into one or more referrals.

We also offer a more lucrative split to the agent if a client returns to do business with them. Providing the agent with a higher split encourages them to do a good job for the clients in order to earn referrals. If the clients are happy with the service they receive, they will recommend our company to friends and family members.

If you offer a 50/50 split, it is hard to attract good agents to your company. Even if you succeed in hiring good agents, they will go back to the offices that offer low fees whenever the market turns around and they don't feel they need your appointments.

If you reward desirable behavior with good appointments and a lucrative split on an agent's referrals, the good agents will prosper and stay with your company. They will tell other good agents about your company and will work to recruit them because we offer the recruiting agent a portion of the gross commission on all of their friend's sales.

We put a lot of effort into making sure that our agents succeed. My brother, Mike, is the Sales Manager in our Residential Sales Division. We pay him a salary and a percentage of the profit from his division. He also sells a few homes each month, which provides him with a third income stream. Before an agent starts with our company, Mike meets with them to determine whether their experience and ethics will be a good fit for our company.

He helps the agents convert their annual income goals into daily actions and trains them on delivering our benefit-rich presentations and performance guarantees. Mike helps the agents make sales forecasts to attain their financial goals and tracks their results to hold them accountable for their goals. We hold sales meetings each week to provide additional training and tools that enable our agents to become more successful.

16

Our New "Pay-to-Play" Plan

Our hybrid solution to commissions, fees, referrals, and bonuses for agents

"I am trying to think of the last time that I just said, 'What the hell!' and did something crazy."– Jennifer Aniston

SOLD ON CHANGE!

We have been experimenting with different ways to pay agents for several years. Prior to 2010, our brokerage was taking 10% off the top of every commission to pay for overhead. We paid the agents 75% of the remaining 90% on sales that came from clients they recruited and 50% of the remaining 90% on the sales that came from clients we attracted. The agents would net 67.5% on sales to their clients (90% X 75% =67.5%) and 45% on sales to our clients (90% X 50% =45%).

By adding an Inside Sales staff, we solved the problem of agents not following up with leads and trying to sell over the phone. In order to improve the conversion of leads to appointments we added several new Inside Sales employees to the payroll and needed to find a way to pay for them.

When we stopped giving leads directly to the agents in May 2009, and began using Inside Sales Associates, we adjusted the agent's pay accordingly. Because call conversion had previously been part of the agent's job, we reduced their split on our leads from 50% to 40% of the commission after deducting the transaction fee. The additional 10% went to pay the ISA staff for setting the appointments.

The commission split to the agents did not change on sales to their referral clients because the ISAs did not set the appointments. In order to pay the ISAs for setting appointments, we reduced the agent's net commission on sales to *our* clients by 9%, from 45% to 36% (90% X 40% = 36%).

Most of our agents did not have many sales to their own clients and were complaining about their net pay. Sale prices had fallen so low that it was getting difficult for us to earn enough to cover our overhead. Both the agents and the company were feeling the pain of having our average commission drop by over 60% in three years. so we had to try something different. We needed to change our compensation plan to reward the agents who sold a lot and to provide a bigger incentive to those who didn't.

We met with the agents in October 2009 to inform them of the changes in compensation that would become effective after the first of the year. To help the agents earn enough to survive, we agreed to reduce the 10% transaction fee in *half*, to only 5% if the agents would charge an additional flat fee commission on each sale. If the agents did not collect the flat fee, we would subtract it from their commission. The fee is needed to help pay for the extra services we provide that other companies don't. To avoid allegations of price-fixing, I cannot disclose the amount of the fee we charge.

Adding a flat fee commission to the commission based on a percentage of the sales price would help compensate for the drastic reduction we were struggling to absorb due to much lower sales prices. For several years, I tried to convince our agents to charge a flat fee in addition to the price-based commission to compensate for the reduced sale prices, but the agents didn't think they would be able to justify it.

It was like waving a magic wand! Suddenly the agents were able to collect the flat fee on every sale! Because the agents could keep any amount over our brokerage minimum, many began to negotiate higher fees for themselves.

At the time, only one of our sales agents was collecting a flat fee and several of our best agents had informed us that their clients would not pay the fee. Since many of our newer agents had recently worked at other companies, I asked each agent how much the other companies were collecting. Although the fees varied widely, most of our competitors were collecting a higher fee than we encouraged our agents to negotiate.

Change in Real Life

<u>Flat Fee Enabler</u>
John Harings, our highest-producing agent sold thirty-seven homes in 2009. Many of the homes he sold were less than $100,000 in value and produced much smaller commission checks than he previously had earned.

To generate more income, John hired an assistant and sold *fifty* homes during the first six months of 2010, mostly in the same low-income neighborhoods.

On average, his gross commission was only $1,800 per home, but the flat fee commission paid in addition to the percentage-based commission offered by the seller enabled him to help the clients purchasing these entry-level homes.

John would not have been able to help his clients or pay his assistant without charging the additional fee for each home he sold.

Our new agent compensation plan became effective January 2010. Agents who were already at our company pay

$1,000 on their credit card on the first of each month. In return for their up-front payment, they receive 95% of the gross commission. The brokerage deducts only 5% of the gross commission in transaction fee plus the flat fee previously discussed, if the agent did not collect it.

We created a second stream of income for those agents who recruited other agents to join our company. The newly recruited agents receive 90% of the gross commission with the extra 5% paid as a bonus to the agent who recruited them to our company.

The agents who were with our company at the time the plan changed earn 5% more than new agents, provided they made the switch to the new plan in January 2010. Since we had not offered a recruiting fee at the time the existing agents were hired, we opted to give the agents the bonus for recruiting themselves into the company. We told them that this was an acknowledgement of their loyalty. The details of the 90/5/5 plan are below:

Monthly Brokerage Fee of $1,000 charged to each agent's credit card on the first business day of each month. Married individuals or business partners who function as a team pay $1,000 for the first agent and $250 for each additional agent. The broker has the final decision as to whether individuals function as a team.

Recruiting Bonus equal to 5% of the gross commission is paid on each transaction to the agent who recruited the new agent to the company. To avoid a bookkeeping nightmare, the bonus is one layer deep. If an agent recruited by someone else recruits an agent to our company, only the agent who recruited the new agent is paid.

We pay only one recruiting bonus per closing. New agents identify in writing which agent was most responsible for their decision to join our company and that agent receives a check every time the new agent sells a home. The bonus is paid on every sale as long as both agents are actively employed at our company and the recruiting agent meets our minimum performance standard.

Transaction Fee equal to 5% of the gross commission earned is charged by the brokerage on each transaction to cover the cost of buying and installing signs & key safes and for the support we provide to manage the listing, offer, and transaction.

Flat Fee Commission specified by the broker is deducted from the agent's portion of the commission on each transaction if the buyer or seller did not pay the fee. Any amount in excess of the broker's established minimum is paid to the agent who negotiated the fee.

Agent Bonuses paid in addition to the gross commission are paid in full to the agent who represented the buyer in the transaction. To qualify for the "pass-through," the bonus must have been offered in writing at the time an offer was accepted.

Agent Commission equal to 90% of the gross commission is paid on each transaction to the agent indicated on the purchase contract provided the agent recruited the client (agents who switched to the new plan in January 2010 receive 95% of the gross commission).

Broker Referral Fee equal to 35% of the gross commission is charged by the brokerage on all transactions in which the clients were procured by broker's goodwill, advertising, systems, or staff.

Minimum Performance Standard is 12 transactions per year per agent. In order to receive a recruiting bonus on another agent's sale, the recruiting agent must have closed at least one transaction in the previous 90 days.

Many of the agents we interview express concern over the monthly $1,000 fee. They often ask whether they can pay the fee out of each commission check rather than on their credit card on the first day of each month. I respond by telling them, "The brokerage fee is a *monthly* fee, not a transactional fee. We do not make special deals for anyone."

I further explain, "Charging a portion of the monthly fee on every transaction would be a bookkeeping nightmare that would turn me into a bill collector rather than a business owner. If you don't think you can earn enough commission to pay a $1,000 monthly fee, I really don't think we want you on our team! We pay our rent, utilities, taxes, advertising and staff wages every month whether we sell any homes or not. When you don't sell to any of the clients we provide to you it hurts the company, so I want it to hurt you too!"

SOLD ON CHANGE!

I remind the agents that if they recruit other agents who together sell four or five homes each month, the recruiting bonuses they earn will offset the $1,000 brokerage fee. If the recruiting income covers the $1,000 brokerage fee and the clients pay the flat fee portion of the commission, our agents receive nearly all of the commission on their sales!

Most agents don't push themselves to sell a home every month, but the $1,000 brokerage fee makes it painful for them not to, so they produce more than they normally would. Some agents will always sell more than others do, but even the low-volume agents seem to work harder when they are keeping more of the money.

I like this plan because the 90% split makes it easier to attract good agents, the 5% recruiting bonus will help retain good agents and their friends, and the monthly brokerage fee will scare off agents who talk a good game but know they will sell only a few homes per year. We earn more, our staff earns more, and the agents earn more because we have established a reward structure in which the agents cannot afford to fail!

With fourteen agents paying the $1,000 brokerage fee up-front, our payroll and overhead is covered on the first of each month without ever selling a home. We distribute each agent's $1,000 brokerage fee payment as follows:

$250 – paid to Outside Sales department to pay for agent training and contract review

$250 – paid to brokerage for overhead (rent on sales building(s), utilities, phones, etc.)

CHAPTER 16 – OUR NEW "PAY-TO-PLAY" PLAN

$500 - paid to Inside Sales department for providing qualified appointments for the agents

This allocation of the broker fee was not random. We know how much we pay the sales manager for training the agents and helping them to establish goals. We also know how much we pay our on-site broker at the sales office to review the contracts. With fourteen agents, we allocate $3,500/mo. ($250 x 14) toward the salary budget for Outside Sales staff members.

As we increase the number of agents in our office, the number of staff members will also need to increase. The additional agents will pay fees that cover the additional salary expense for the Outside Sales staff.

We also know how much the building rent, utilities, phones, and other overhead costs each month. With fourteen agents, we allocate $3,500/mo. ($250 x 14) toward the Overhead budget. As we increase the number of agents in our office, the need will arise for additional space. The additional agents will pay fees that cover the additional overhead associated with more space and higher overhead costs.

The one thing that we didn't know is how much it would cost to meet our goal of setting an average of two appointments per agent per week on average for those on this fee plan. With fourteen agents, we allocate $7,000/mo. ($500 x 14) toward the Inside Sales budget. As we increase the number of agents in our office, the need will arise for additional employees to set more and more appointments each week. The additional agents will pay fees that cover the salaries of additional Inside Sales staff members.

To determine a budget for the Inside Sales Department we multiply the total number of agents by the number of appointments we expect per agent per week. In this example, we have 14 agents and expect two appointments per agent per week, or 28 total appointments per week (14 x 2 = 28).

To calculate the number of appointments we need to set in a month we need to multiply by 52 weeks in a year and then divide by twelve months (28 X 52 = 1,456 / 12 = 121.33). We need an average of 121.33 appointments per month. Since in this example we allocated $7,000 toward setting 121 appointments, we can determine that our cost per appointment cannot exceed $57.69 (7,000 / 121.33 = 57.69).

Although the previous pay plan was discontinued when the new plan was adopted, we temporarily allowed our legacy agents to remain on the old plan if they didn't opt to change to the new plan. All agents hired after the new plan was introduced are on the new plan, but we added a second plan to accommodate the squeamish agents who just could not commit to the $1,000 plan.

The second plan requires agents to pay only $500 via credit card on the first of each month. Instead of a 90% split, agents on the $500 plan receive 78% on their referral business. The brokerage charges a 35% referral fee on all referrals, which leaves the agents 43% of the gross commission, 7% more than the 36% they previously received on the legacy plan.

CHAPTER 16 – OUR NEW "PAY-TO-PLAY" PLAN

In an effort to keep the agents from trying to game the system, they are only allowed to switch plans once per year. We require a 60-day written notice prior to the plan change. All transactions under contract at the time of the written notice are calculated and paid using the plan the agent was on at the time the contracts were initiated. Appointments set prior to the change are paid using the pay plan in effect at the time the appointment was set.

17

Outstanding Outcome
The results of our new agent pay plan and who <u>not</u> to hire as Sales Manager

"I have not failed. I've just found 10,000 ways that won't work."– Thomas Alva Edison

The new plan was slow to take off during the first three months. We analyzed our overhead and knew that we needed at least ten agents paying $1,000 for the new pay plan to work. Many of the agents we initially thought were switching got cold feet and backed out. When we showed them how it could more than double their income, our three best agents made the plunge and have been taking home thousands more each month because of their production.

Initially, this was a huge hit to our bottom line. We operated at a loss for a few months while we added more agents, but after the fourth month, we had ten agents on the new plan and by the sixth month, we had fourteen agents paying the up-front fee.

I now spend significantly less time recruiting new agents. Since we began paying our agents a percentage of the commission earned by the agents they recruit, the agents have recruited more than half of the new agents on our team!

They don't recruit slackers who won't produce very many sales, but a few agents have paid the brokerage fee for their friends for a few months while their pipeline becomes full. We hold an orientation class once each month to train new agents but we have begun to record all of our training and orientation sessions to enable agents to join our team in between orientation sessions.

We are now converting three times more callers than when the agents received the leads directly. We are also doing a much better job of incubating the callers who are not ready to act so we will get their business when they are ready. We track the origin of each lead so we know that our incubation process is working! Several clients who initially called our office in 2009 eventually bought or sold homes with us in 2010.

After closing only 45 transactions during the first half of 2009, our agents, staff, and systems have improved drastically. At one point in June 2010, we had 134 properties under contract at the same time. The fourteen agents in our residential division had 68 of the sales, an average of *five* sales per agent!

We had initially set the minimum performance standard for agents at 18 sales per year. We later determined that the goal was too aggressive so we lowered the minimum to 12 sales per agent per year. I am usually not one to lower my expectations but selling 12 homes per year is *six times* more than the average agent sells in a year, so we decided to cut the agents a little slack! Besides, we have four agents who may sell enough to bring the team average to 18 sales anyway.

It never ceases to amaze me how some people seize an opportunity and propel themselves to unbelievable success while others with the same opportunity do just enough to get by and complain about the outcome.

We are on track to sell over 300 homes in our Residential division in 2010. The agents who have joined our team are selling far more than they could sell on their own. Nearly two-thirds of the agents' sales come from the appointments set by our Inside Sales team.

SOLD ON CHANGE!

We pay 20% of our profit in bonuses to our staff. This keeps the advertising and appointments flowing smoothly. Two members of our Inside Sales staff worked a booth over the weekend at a recent festival. During the two-day event, they signed up more than 60 new prospects! Both employees are salaried so we paid them for their extra effort, but you just have to appreciate their creativity. If you want your business to take a quantum leap like ours has, set up a pay plan where extra effort is rewarded and everyone wins!

Costly Promotion

John Harings has been the most productive agent in our brokerage since I stopped working directly with clients. Before getting his real estate license, he was one of our best clients. When we began to get too many agents for me to manage, we decided to promote John, an Associate Broker to the position of Sales Manager. Although John was reliable and did a great job, it was not a good move for him or us.

John went from selling eight homes each month to selling only two per month as more and more of his time was used to train other agents. We not only experienced a huge loss in our income, we had to pay him a salary for helping other agents. The salary he received wasn't as much as he'd been making selling homes so it wasn't good for him either. Within two months, we mutually agreed to switch him back to his previous position as a sales agent before either of us lost any more money.

126

CHAPTER 17 – Outstanding Outcome

When you have a top producer who is good at sales, don't bog them down with management duties. If anything, encourage them to hire an assistant so they can produce more sales in less time. John consistently writes more offers and sells more homes than anyone else on the team. The other agents in our office treat him like a rock star because they all aspire to be like him someday. John attends every weekly meeting and provides help to the other agents when they need it. His success as a peer motivates the other agents more than if John was their manager.

Making your best agent a sales manager is a huge mistake that will cost *both* of you tens of thousands of dollars. If you don't remedy the situation quickly, you may lose your star agent to a better split at another company.

18

Attracting Agents
How to recruit and hire top-producing agents who are not at their full potential

"Whether you think you can or think you can't, either way you are right."– Henry Ford

SOLD ON CHANGE!

The best way to recruit motivated agents is to let them know you have more business than you can handle. We target agents who sold 12 to 20 homes during the previous year. The fact that these agents sold several times more than the national average shows they are hard workers, they have experience, and they are good at selling!

In Figure 18-1 I've included a sample of the recruiting flyer we use for this event. The e-mail we send to invite agents to our recruiting events is provided in Figure18-2.

Figure 18-1 Recruiting Seminar Flyer

Win3 Realty
Agent Opportunities Seminar

Come and See....
Why our agents are **WINNING!**
- OVER 200 *NEW* Buyer Calls/Internet Leads Per Week
- FULL Support Staff and APPOINTMENTS provided to agents
- EXPERIENCE & PROVEN Track Record of Success

Win3 Realty
Closed 502 Homes in 2009 and
Over 300 from Jan - May 2010!

Monday, June 14, 2010
5:30 - 6:30 PM
(Stay after for Q & A)

Win3 Realty Sales Office
(123 E. Main St. Tucson, AZ 85XXX)
Light refreshments will be provided

RSVP: agentsevent@win3realty.com
or
Call (520) XXX-XXXX

Figure 18-2 Recruiting Seminar E-mail

Hello!

I wanted to invite you to an informational session about agent opportunities at Win3 Realty on **Monday, June 14th at 5:30 PM**.

Our small team currently has **68 buyer-side transactions in escrow** and we receive more than 200 buyer calls per week!

The meeting will be held at 123 E. Main Street Tucson , AZ

Please bring an   *open mind* and a *friend*
(you could receive 5% of the gross commission on everything they sell!)

RSVP to agentsevent@win3realty.com or call **(520) XXX-XXXX**

Thanks!

Bob Zachmeier
Broker/Owner - Win3 Realty
Tucson, AZ

We personally contact the agents by telephone to invite them to a recruiting event with no more than four other agents invited. We tell the agents we would like to show them how to *double* the amount they earned during the previous year

We start the presentation by showing several charts and graphs to illustrate what is happening in the local market. We inform the agents that if they worked at our company they could have access to the same charts to educate *their* clients. We end the chart portion of the presentation by showing them how the market supply has returned to normal levels after nearly doubling in 2006 and 2007. We ask the agents whether their real estate sales are back to normal.

Next, we show them why short sales will be prevalent in our marketplace until prices appreciate at least another thirty to forty percent. After pointing out the negative aspects of working on short sales I ask them how many they could work on concurrently. We inform the agents that we have an entire division dedicated to short sales and explain how they could hand off their file after their first appointment, let us negotiate the short sale for them, and still receive 25% of the commission.

We next educate them about the downsides of selling REO properties by sharing how much we have outstanding in utility and repair bills and how many staff members we need to employ in order to get everything done. We then inform them of the upside of selling REO properties, the sign calls. We tell them about the 200 buyer calls to our office each week, how we determine which clients are ready to act, and how we set appointments for our agents with the clients who are ready.

At this point, I provide our company history, share our "no negativity" philosophy, and explain why their child's soccer games and school plays should be considered "appointments" and never be cancelled. Then we share some of the technology we employ to make their job easier and explain how much spare time they will have because our staff is performing all of the tasks that don't require a real estate license.

We explain the compensation plan like this, "Five percent of the gross commission goes to the agent who brought you into our company and five percent goes to the office for buying and installing the signs and key safes and for handling all of the paperwork on your transactions. Ninety percent of the gross commission goes to you."

"In the event your referral business gets slow, we will set appointments with clients for you at our office. A thirty-five percent referral fee is charged for appointments screened and set by our staff, which is business you wouldn't otherwise have. Other companies charge more than that for just a name and phone number. We're setting an appointment with a person willing to drive across town to meet with you!"

To minimize the impact of our brokerage fee, we follow with, "If the agents you recruit sell several homes each month, the recruiting fee you receive from their sales could be enough to offset your monthly brokerage fee. All that you will be paying us is the 5% for signs, key safes, and travel that you would have to pay for anyway. And, if you recruit enough agents, you can earn more than $1,000 in referral fees!"

We end the presentation with a summary of the benefits of working at our company. A partial list is provided below:

- REO properties to sell to buyers!
- Full-time advertising manager
- Full-time lead coordinator
- Sales Manager for weekly training/personal coaching
- Average of more than 200 leads per week
- Free advertising to those in your "sphere of influence"
- Free sign printing and installation
- Free key safes, installation, and key copies

- MLS entry and updates done for you
- No broker deduction on agent bonuses
- Offer Dept. to review and track deadlines
- Listing Dept. to update clients with internet hits and comps
- Automated showing feedback with 24/7 access for clients
- Transaction Dept, updates agents, title company, & lender every three days, tracks status, issues cure notices, ensures that all documents are on time and accurate

When we held our first recruiting seminar, five agents showed up and two of them joined our team. I created a quick presentation prior to the meeting and didn't do much else other than approve the list of agents who were invited to attend. Our Residential division support staff took care of everything else. I *love* sharing our profit with a staff that *gets* it! All I had to do was show up!

We pay the agents their commission checks at the weekly sales meetings and make a big deal out of those receiving "free money" without having sold anything. I've been thinking about playing the Dire Straits song, "Money for Nothing" while the referral checks are being distributed. When your agents start receiving 5% of the commission on homes sold by their friends, they will be doing all of the recruiting for you!

In closing the recruitment presentation, I explain what being a team player means like this, "If you are an agent on the Win3 Realty team, our systems and sales statistics will help you attract more business. Our team generates all of the advertising, answers and screens all the calls, and sets all the appointments.

The team also completes the MLS input and installs the signs, key safes, and sign riders. Our team handles all the paperwork while the property is listed, forwards offers and counter-offers during negotiation, and manages the transaction until closing, calling the Buyer's lender and Title Company for you. When the property is finally closed, it is a *team sale*.

When you go to a baseball game, they don't have a separate scoreboard for each player. There is only one scoreboard for the entire team. If you're going to benefit from using the statistics of our team, you have to give credit to the team when a property sells!"

19

Ramping Up for REO

How to departmentalize your real estate team for efficiency, accuracy, and volume

"Efficiency is doing things right. Effectiveness is doing the right things."– Peter Drucker

When a bank forecloses on a property, they refer to the properties on their balance sheet as *real estate owned* or "REO." If your brokerage is hired by a bank or outsourcing company to sell their foreclosed properties you'll need to hire additional staff members for positions that are not typically found on a real estate team.

Once you are assigned properties to sell, most banks and outsourcing companies will provide you with access to a secure website, a portal to their online database. This is how the bank client and you will track the history and status of each property being sold. These systems automatically assign new tasks to the listing agent as the property progresses through the sales process.

For instance, when a property is first assigned you'll receive a task to verify whether the property is occupied. If you log into the client's portal and indicate that the property is vacant, you'll immediately be assigned new tasks to re-key the locks, activate utilities, initiate lawn service (or snow removal), and obtain Home Owners Association information.

If you indicate that the property is occupied, you'll receive a task to upload the occupants name and contact information and to negotiate a "relocation agreement" with the occupants, commonly referred to as a "Cash for Keys" agreement. Selling foreclosed homes can be very stressful because every time one task is completed two or three more are immediately spawned.

CHAPTER 19 – RAMPING UP FOR REO

Currently, Win3 Realty represents several bank clients selling REO properties. Because of the large number of properties we are handling for these banks and outsourcing companies, we sometimes receive more than 600 e-mails per day related to the various tasks assigned to us for each property.

While your volume may not reach this level, if you decide to handle REO sales, you'll still need reliable people to ensure that each task for a property is completed correctly, in a workman-like manner, and that the client's online portal is updated in a timely manner.

As the volume of your REO listings grows, the number of staff members assisting you will need to increase accordingly. Since these positions require a lot of training, you'll need to be prompt about hiring additional staff!

Our REO Division is one of five divisions of our business (see Chapter 9 – "Branches of Business"). Within the REO division, we've created several teams to complete work that is not typical in real estate sales for traditional buyers and sellers. At times, some of these team members provide services to other divisions in our business. When this happens, their time is accounted for accordingly.

Teams within our REO Division are:
• <u>Upload team</u> - Uploads required documents for each property to client's online portal
• <u>Dispatch team</u> - schedules physical visits to the properties

- <u>Courier team</u> - verifies occupancy, physical condition, and whether repair quotes might be necessary
- <u>BPO team</u> - assists the broker in preparing a *broker price opinion* by inputting data, uploading photos, and obtaining information from the MLS and tax assessor websites
- <u>Repair team</u> - obtains contractor quotes and coordinates all repairs and maintenance
- <u>Bookkeeping/Accounting team</u> - processes and uploads invoices and copies of the corresponding checks for reimbursement of all expenses paid by the broker on REO properties

<u>Upload Team</u> - Tasks to provide required documentation such as purchase agreements, addendums, contractor quotes and photos, etc. to the seller are sent to our "REO Upload" team. As each document is uploaded via the client's portal into their database, the corresponding e-mail for that task is deleted from the REO task queue. This ensures that the work is not duplicated by another employee.

<u>Dispatch Team</u> - Tasks that require travel to a property are sent to our dispatch team. At the end of each day, all of the tasks sent to dispatch team are placed on a courier's schedule for the following day.

<u>Courier Team</u> - We have two full-time staff members, couriers, in the field at all times conducting property checks to ensure that the properties assigned to us are secure and in good condition. On some visits, the couriers verify that repairs have been completed appropriately and take photos of the finished work. They take new photos of the homes during each visit and complete a checklist to verify that each property is being presented as favorably as possible to potential buyers.

If there is trash in the yard, newspapers on the doorstep, or cobwebs in the entry the couriers remove them before leaving the property. They also replace light bulbs that are not functioning properly and pour Pine-Sol® cleaner down the drain to kill bacteria and alleviate any odors from expanding sewer gas, especially in the summer months.

Broker Price Opinion – BPO Team - Before listing a foreclosed property for sale, most of our bank clients hire an appraiser and two real estate brokers to give them an opinion of value. An appraisal follows a specific set of rules to estimate the value of a property based on other sales of similar homes in the area. An appraisal looks *backward* in time.

A broker price opinion (BPO) is based on comparisons of three active properties (currently listed for sale on the MLS) and three sold properties that are similar in size and age to the subject property. A BPO is a *forward-looking* opinion of value based on what the broker believes the property could be sold for during a specific future time frame.

Most bank clients request that the broker provide a ninety-day value. This is the broker's opinion of the list price that would attract an offer in 90 days or less. Some bank clients might request a thirty-day value to sell the property quickly. The price opinion must be adjusted higher or lower to meet the client's requirements. Usually, the price must be adjusted lower for a shorter marketing time.

When bank clients assign a property to an REO broker, the broker must provide a BPO at the time the property is listed and an additional report each month the property is on the market to inform the client of any recent sales or new properties that might have been listed. The monthly report is similar to a BPO but is called a *monthly status report* (MSR).

Each new BPO or MSR requires a trip to the property for photos, as well as information about three similar properties that have recently been sold and three that are actively for sale, comparing the amenities of each nearby property to those of the subject property.

The timeliness and accuracy of your BPOs and MSRs will affect how many REO properties a bank client will assign to you. Most clients grade your performance based on how close your initial BPO estimate is to the actual selling price. While you can hire staff members to help find comparable properties and to take photos, the analysis should always be done by you or another agent on your staff who has a firm grasp of what's happening in the local market and in the specific neighborhood where each property is located. Your BPO is your calling card so it pays to take the time to be right and to meet deadlines!

Repair Team - Many times when you list a client's properties they will ask your advice on repairs that should be completed prior to the property being listed for sale. Properties with obvious defects will not sell as quickly as properties that are in good condition. Before making repairs, the sellers need to consider whether the cost of the repair might be recovered by a higher sales price or a shorter marketing time.

On most bank-owned properties, the listing agent is responsible for getting all of the repair bids, uploading the bid estimates to the client's portal, and then arranging for the work to be done and *paying* for the repairs after the client approves them. You also will be required to initiate all utility services in your name and pay the monthly gas, water, and electric bills for the properties until they sell.

The banks will reimburse the expenses if the invoice and a copy of the check you used to pay the bill are submitted in a timely manner. Reimbursement can take several months, so we allocate about $1,500 per property in available cash or credit.

Besides opening lines of credit at local banks and asking to have your credit card limits raised, you'll need to employ staff members to meet with contractors at the properties, obtain cost estimates, and inspect the work after the repairs have been completed. This requires a large financial commitment and additional employees that aren't required with conventional real estate sales.

Rather than spending their own money on repairs, some REO agents advise their clients that it would be best to sell the homes assigned to them in "AS-IS" condition. This may save the REO listing agent an outlay of cash to pay for the repairs in the short-term, but they run the risk of being fired by their bank client.

SOLD ON CHANGE!

Those who are not fired will lose tens of thousands because properties sell faster and for more money when they are repaired and in good condition. Since most bank clients place caps on the number of properties they will assign to you at any given time, money spent on repairs helps the properties sell faster, which leads to more assignments from the client. You will also receive higher commissions because the repaired properties will sell at higher prices.

It is very shortsighted to try to save money by not activating the utilities or not doing necessary repairs. Many banks and outsourcing companies have begun to hire "secret shoppers" to conduct inspections on their listed properties. Saving a few thousand dollars is not worth losing a client that could provide you with twenty-five or more commission checks per year!

If you wish to sell REO properties, be prepared to front the money and time to make repairs and pay for utilities until the property sells.

Bookkeeping/Accounting Team - One of the most important persons in your REO Division is your bookkeeper. Be sure to hire a bookkeeper to submit the repair bills and utilities as quickly as you receive them. Be sure to choose someone who is reliable, can be trusted, and pays attention to details. Most of our clients require expenses to be submitted within a week or two of the work being done. Mistakes in this department could result in tens of thousands of dollars in lost revenue.

Change in Real Life

<u>Bookkeepers are Free!</u>

During 2008 we lost more than $70,000 in unreimbursed expenses on our REO properties. Some of the loss is expected due to utility company billing cycles, but much of the loss was caused by reimbursement requests being submitted too late.

This was a huge mistake! Hiring a full-time bookkeeper would have cost less than $30,000 and would have saved us from personally uploading all of the bills for reimbursement.

In 2009 we sold more than twice as many bank-owned properties but lost only about half as much in unreimbursed expenses. Kay Reed, our bookkeeper, and Tina Hoffman in our Billing Department have done an excellent job of handling reimbursements!

We know that we'll probably not be reimbursed for the final gas, electric, and water bills for the properties we sell because the bills will arrive after the submission deadline. Utility companies have a specific billing cycle and usually are unwilling to generate a separate bill that will arrive in time to be reimbursed by the bank seller.

We expect to lose about $200 on every bank-owned property that we sell. If you had a client who was selling multiple homes you'd probably give them a commission discount of at least that much. We view the loss as just another cost of doing business.

20

Satisfying REO Sellers

How to manage repairs, broker price opinions, and local lender performance

"Earth provides enough to satisfy every man's need, but not every man's greed."– Mahatma Gandhi

Repairs and Reimbursements

If you have any REO relationships with banks, don't neglect your property preservation services! When you receive new property assignments, quickly activate utilities, order lawn service, and complete necessary repairs. We have set up credit lines, obtained additional credit cards and, occasionally, borrowed in order to spend as much as $50,000 per week repairing bank-owned properties. We carry an ever-increasing amount of bank debt.

Most of the bank clients we work with really watch out for the brokers handling their properties by trying to process reimbursements as quickly as possible. However, some unscrupulous companies attempt to create a new profit center by cheating their REO brokers out of reimbursements for repairs they authorized. One such company refused to repay us even though we could prove in their own system that our bills were submitted on time! We fired them!

No matter how "good" a client is or *was*, when they owe you more than you earn by selling their properties, they become a "bad" client. If a bank client's asset manager or operations manager won't stand up for you, my advice is to quit while you're ahead. Reputation is everything in this business.

News of a company's unfair reimbursement policies will travel to other REO brokers and soon, *good* agents will not work for them. The profit these rogue companies collect by cheating REO agents is lost when they are fired by their clients for providing poor service with unqualified agents.

CHAPTER 20 – SATISFYING REO SELLERS

Broker Price Opinions (BPOs)

The accuracy of the initial price opinion can account for as much as 80% of your vendor scorecard. You should <u>never</u> delegate the pricing decision due to the importance of this task and the sensitivity of the asset manager's personal contact information.

Before giving an opinion of value, you really need to understand your bank client's sales goal. Some REO companies want to have their properties sold in 30 days or less and others try to obtain a higher value by waiting 90 days or more for a sale. Some bank clients are willing to wait even longer in an attempt to hold neighborhood values high.

An opinion of value can vary greatly between a 30-day sale and a 90-day sale. When only 8% of all actively-listed homes are selling each month, how aggressive should the list price be to attract an offer? When 92% of the listed properties are <u>not</u> selling, how much will you have to reduce the price to sell the property in 30 days?

You must know the target your bank clients expect so you can adjust the price accordingly. When in doubt, put yourself in the bank's position. Determine what you would do if the property were your personal residence and you needed to sell it in 30 days.

For properties that are listed, the bank client will usually require monthly status reports (MSRs), which are similar to BPOs. One of the biggest mistakes you can make with a BPO or MSR for a property already listed is to arrive at a value that is *higher* than the current list price. Bank asset managers fire people over this! Always compare the recommended price to the asking price before sending it to your asset manager. It could keep you from losing a client!

We use a program called BPO Genius™ to track all of the BPO and MSR assignments in our company. The software "dashboard" sorts the tasks in the order they are due and quickly shows the status of each task. The time stamp cannot be changed so there is no way for your employees to game the system by saying they are done with a task and then coming back later to finish it. Client contact information is protected so unauthorized users cannot gain access to the system or and try to steal business from you later.

BPO Genius provides reports that show the outstanding payments due, the number of orders received from each client, and the average price paid on each order. The reports will tally the properties each employee worked on so your bookkeeper can easily pay them for their work.

We usually carry about 300 REO properties at a time. Although this may sound lucrative, it can also be expensive. Besides paying the repairs and utilities, each property requires either a BPO or MSR each month. We typically receive $50 to prepare these reports, but when we list a property, the reports are considered part of the responsibility of managing the listing. With 300 listings, if we were paid $50 for every BPO or MSR we create, we would earn an extra $15,000 per <u>month</u>! It can be expensive if your properties don't sell! This is another reason why it's so important to have accurate BPOs.

I've heard many agents describe a BPO as a mini-appraisal, but I disagree! Most appraisers are not actively involved in selling homes so they cannot measure market sentiment as well as a real estate broker who is out with clients every day. A BPO is a *forward-looking* estimate of what a broker *believes* a property could sell for based on current buyer sentiment.

Appraisals don't take into account seasonal changes, loan programs, or interest rates, which have a lot to do with how much a potential buyer will pay in the next 90 days. Although most banks acquire both appraisals and BPOs, some financial institutions place more weight on the BPO value. It seems logical to get the value from the person who has to *sell* the property in the future.

Controlling Non-Performing Lenders

During the past few years, some of our REO properties have been reassigned to other brokers when the Buyer's local lender failed to fund a loan after months of extensions and reassurances. To reduce the number of transactions that don't close on time we've enacted the following procedures:

1) We inform the Buyer's agents in advance to avoid closing during the last three days of the month. We ask that they move the closing either forward a week or back a week, to ensure that a small delay won't push the closing from one month to another.

2) We started a "Lender Wall of Shame" in our office that has the name and photo of the Buyer's lenders who have demonstrated that they cannot close loans on time. When a loan does not close on schedule due to delays from the Buyer's lender, we add their name to our wall. We telephone the lender to tell them that their name is on our "Wall of Shame" and inform them that if they miss another closing date they will be moved to our "DO NOT USE" (DNU) list.

If a future offer comes into our office with a loan qualification letter from a lender on the DNU list, we notify our Seller client that the lender has a history of not closing on time. Each client decides whether to move forward with the offer or decline it. Some of our clients thank us for telling them about the local lender's history and decline the offer. When this happens, we notify the Buyer's agent and inform them that the Buyer's offer would be reconsidered if they found a different lender.

3) Several banks require that a loan qualification letter from their institution be submitted with all offers on their REO properties. Besides helping them to determine whether the potential buyers are qualified before taking a property off the market, it also gives them an opportunity to compete for the buyer's loan business.

21

REO Tips
and Techniques

How to sell for higher prices, make the most
of REO conferences, and handle being sued

"The secret of success is to know something nobody else knows."– Aristotle Onassis

The Escalator Clause

In 2005, most newly listed homes in Tucson were sold within a matter of hours for well over the asking price. Many of our clients submitted offers higher than the asking price on the first day a property appeared on the MLS, only to find that their offer was beaten by an offer that was ten or twenty thousand dollars higher! The prices being paid were not logical, but some buyers seemed to care more about winning than how much they paid!

An *escalator clause* provides a way to win a bidding war without significantly overpaying for a property. The clause simply states, "Buyer to pay $1,000 more than highest verified offer, up to a maximum of $250,000." In situations where two offers used an escalator clause, the bidding simply goes back and forth much like an auction until one offer reaches the high-end limit and the other goes $1,000 higher.

Many agents in Tucson revived the escalator clause in 2008 when bidding wars occurred on our REO properties. Some REO agents do not acknowledge escalator clauses and simply input the buyer's starting bid. The job of a listing agent is to do what is best for the Seller. Offers with an escalator clause will usually net the Seller more money than they would otherwise receive. These offers can help to stabilize falling property values and should be utilized whenever possible.

When you write an offer with an escalator clause for a buyer, be sure to follow up with the listing agent. Make sure that they understand the concept and are willing to use a calculator to determine the winning offer. If there are multiple offers and the REO listing agent submits your offer at the lowest value, your client will lose the home to another buyer.

Escalator clauses can benefit sellers because many times buyers will bid much higher than the asking price. In these situations, the Seller often times selects a *cash* offer to avoid appraisal issues later (cash offers don't require an appraisal).

Change in Real Life

REO Reassignments

Sometimes a bank-owned property initially assigned to one broker is re-assigned to other REO broker. It happens to all REO brokers, (sometimes you wind up on the receiving end).

We recently received a $400,000 property that had been assigned to another agent. The agent spent more than $5,000 in repairs and was very frustrated. She informed me that three offers had been submitted by other agents, even though the property was not yet listed.

I asked her to send the offers to me and promised to pay her a 25% referral fee if any of them was accepted and closed. It made her day! One of the offers was accepted and we paid her as promised when the transaction closed.

You should be fair with other agents in your market. It will come back to you some day. When you treat people fairly and honor your word, they will respect you.

Attending Conferences

In 2009, I attended as many REO conferences as I could fit into my schedule and acquired several new clients. I especially like approaching the companies that say they are not hiring. You are not likely to get an account with REO companies by applying online and waiting.

You have to stand out from your competitors and meeting lenders face-to-face is the best way to win REO business. You have to sell bank clients on the services you can offer them and be ready to prove it!

Change in Real Life

Keynote Speaker or Key REO Account?

I once met a regional manager from a very large national bank in the Exposition Hall at a conference while everyone else was listening to the keynote speaker. Although I would have enjoyed listening to Bill Rancic, the first Apprentice of Donald Trump, I was there to learn and network.

At conferences, I get up early, stay up late, and take tons of notes so when I returned home we can implement as much as possible before the next conference opportunity.

Because of that meeting with the regional manager, I became a preferred broker with the bank and have received more than 150 properties from them thus far. It paid, to skip the keynote speaker!

Asset Managers need to know what is happening in local markets. I prepare market charts for the companies I already work for and show them to the companies where I would like to be hired. All sellers, even banks, want buyers. Show them that you have buyers and you will get their business!

If you teach your clients about what is happening in the market, they will be better prepared for negotiating offers with buyers or sellers. Most agents don't provide the data that we do. When sellers want to overprice their home we go back to the charts and show them the data and what the market will bear. This is just as effective with REO clients as it is with traditional real estate clients.

Commercial REO

Several bank clients have made the decision <u>not</u> to open a commercial REO division because they expect the commercial downturn to last only a few years. Rather than sell the commercial assets they acquire at the market bottom, some financial institutions have opted to hire commercial management companies to rent the properties until the commercial market improves.

If you are planning to open a Commercial REO division in your company, be aware that many bank clients look for commercial REO brokers with a CCIM designation. To achieve this certification you must take a series of classes and close $10M in commercial property sales and leases. Some banks reportedly seek to hire CCIM brokers with $50M or more in commercial sales experience.

SOLD ON CHANGE!

By mid-2010, over 700 banks were on the FDIC's "watch list." If a bank falls below the required capital requirement, the FDIC issues a warning letter. Banks receiving the warning letter either make a capital call to their investors for an immediate deposit of more money or they must sell off some of their non-performing assets. Either of these things must happen very quickly or the bank could be shut down!

When banks have to sell assets quickly, they use a Loan Sale Advisor who coordinates the sale via a network of cash investors. Sources tell me that the big bulk deals usually carry price tags with nine zeros (one billion) and consist of properties located all over the nation. The cash is placed in a local trust account with 10% of the funds wired to the bank before you can bid. If you lose the bid they refund your money, but the deposit is non-refundable, so if they select your bid and you don't follow through and buy the assets, you lose the 10% earnest money of *$100 Million Dollars!* This is clearly not a game for local investors.

The *national* buyers have a *regional* network of buyers who cover a four or five state area. The assets in that region sell within a few days of the bulk sale. The *regional* buyers sell within a few days to buyers who only want properties in their own *state*. The *state* buyers sell assets in a specific metropolitan area to *local* buyers. This is the "retail" price of commercial deals in your local market. Apparently, the majority of this activity occurs at the end of the bank's fiscal quarter, so start pooling your money!

There are billions in profit realized in the commercial arena every day. The sad truth is that politicians and the media do not seem to care if a business owner loses their business or if an investor loses their apartment building. There will be no *crisis*. Without government intervention, the free market will consume the failed deal, it will change owners three or four times within a month, and then it will be *gone!*

Get Used To Being Sued

With success comes attention, and not all of it is good. For some reason, being successful causes people who are not successful to sue you. Many people freak out when they receive a letter from an attorney but unfortunately, I've gotten used to it.

People hire an attorney to write a letter rather than writing it themselves for the *shock* effect. Having your attorney respond to the letter usually puts an end to most of these issues because the people frivolously suing you don't want to spend any more money on what they know is probably a lost cause.

The frequency of such lawsuits has increased since the advent of prepaid legal services but most claims have no merit and will go away with time. You will usually prevail if you can provide a timeline, written documentation, and an e-mail trail.

The public perceives foreclosed homes as a good deal, just as everyone expects to find lower prices at an auction sale than in a retail store. For this reason, multiple offers commonly occur on newly-listed foreclosure properties. We have had as many as 22 offers on one property. This is not a good situation because only one person wins and everyone else is angry.

Change in Real Life

Sued For Doing Your Job!

A few years ago, a desirable REO property attracted multiple offers and ended up selling for $50,000 higher than the list price. A week before the property was due to close, we learned that the appraiser had valued the property $20,000 lower than the contract price. Even if the Seller had opted to accept the next highest offer, the appraisal would likely have been less than that offer too. Rather than start the process over, the bank opted to reduce the sale price to the appraised value.

Shortly after the sale price was recorded in the MLS, other agents who had submitted offers on the property began to call. Then a registered letter from an attorney arrived. The situation could have been upsetting, but we knew that we had followed our client's direction and had not done anything wrong.

After providing proof that the Seller had received all of the offers and had selected the offer of the Buyer who ultimately purchased the property, the issue went away.

My friend, Tim Burrell in Raleigh, North Carolina, is a real estate broker, author, and as he likes to say, "A recovering California attorney." Tim gave some good advice to another friend recently in a message posted on REObroker.com. Tim's message is reprinted with permission below:

"Do not give the letter the opportunity to upset you. The negotiating strategy is to have you want to get out of this troubling situation, so you will give them more than they are entitled to. You get letters every day. Some are from friends that make you happy; some are from business situations that upset you. This one is from an attorney, and it is just another letter. If you give it the power to upset you, you will change your professional response. Just take it in stride. This is just another negotiating situation that will have to be worked out."

22

Succeeding at Short Sales

How to compensate your staff and create a fee-based short sale model for your clients

"People fail forward to success." – Mary Kay Ash

SOLD ON CHANGE!

A *short sale* occurs when a lien holder agrees to allow a homeowner to sell their house "short" of what is owed. If you have not started a Short Sale division in your real estate company, you should do it <u>now</u>! The government and the banks are doing everything they can to stop foreclosures, but millions of short sales will occur in the markets that experienced several years of unsustainable appreciation.

In a recent study, Wachovia Bank found that they saved $38,000 per loan by working with homeowners to complete a short sale rather than foreclosing on their home. In a short sale situation, the bank saves time and labor compared to a foreclosure, pays lower attorney fees, and seldom is asked to make repairs on the property. Since the homeowners often live in the home until closing, they pay their own utility bills, and the occurrence of vandalism is much lower with the homeowner living in the property.

Experience has taught me that listing short sales often means higher sales prices, better commission rates, and far less labor-intensive tasks than listing REO properties. The best part is that you don't have to spend any of your own money on repairs, utilities, or "cash-for-keys" payments.

Our first short sale in 2007 was a disaster! The short sale went through and our clients avoided foreclosure, but it was not pretty! We lost two qualified buyers during the six months it took to close. The final selling price was $25,000 lower than the initial buyer's offer because the home was dropping hundreds of dollars in value each day.

When the short sale approval letter finally arrived, the bank conveniently used the property tax and HOA payoff estimates from the original HUD1 closing statement that was submitted six months earlier.

I gave up a good portion of my commission to make up the difference and the title company reduced some of their fees to help make up the shortage. On the day of closing, the second mortgage holder dropped a bombshell. After the Buyer and Seller had signed all the closing documents, the second mortgage holder decided that the amount they had initially agreed to accept was no longer enough to satisfy them. The Loss Mitigator for the second mortgage holder increased the payoff amount from $1,000 to 10,000.

After three days of speaking with an arrogant Loss Mitigator in another country, I finally got a reasonable Loss Mitigator to settle for $2,000 rather than the $10,000 her colleague had insisted on. We were on the verge of losing our third buyer for this property and I was so ready for the ordeal to be over that I allowed them to take the extra $1,000 out of my commission too. I now know that many loss mitigation companies rely on this strategy but I don't fall for that tactic anymore.

I vowed to never again participate in a situation in which I did not have a way to win. I attended a short sale boot camp and spent $16,000 on a short sale coaching program. After the training we began closing our short sales much faster and without sacrificing half of our commission in the process.

Short sales were very unpredictable until mid-2009 when the mortgage industry finally got enough people and systems in place to process the unprecedented number of upside-down homeowners. We hired a full-time salaried broker to staff our Short Sale division and sent her to the same training that I had taken. In addition to her monthly salary, she shares in a portion of the profit from the Short Sale division.

The legal instrument most commonly used to begin a foreclosure is a Notice of Default (NOD). Most counties publish a list of foreclosure filings in a local newspaper to satisfy the requirement of public notice. Many investors and real estate agents attempt to contact the people in default with postcards, letters, telephone calls, or by knocking on their door.

Door knocking often yields the best results but can be dangerous at times. I do not recommend sending postcards because many homeowners get upset if their children and the mail carrier learn that they may be behind on their payments. A short, hand-written letter is the best way to attract short sale clients. Writing the letters by hand may sound time-consuming, but if you have each member of your staff write five letters per day it goes very quickly.

Many people in a short sale situation are in denial. Ads directed toward them are not nearly as effective as ads in the third person. Use ads that ask, "Do you *know of* someone in danger of losing their home?" Then pile on the testimonials from other clients whom you have successfully helped avoid foreclosure.

CHAPTER 22 – SUCCEEDING AT SHORT SALES

People who call our office speak directly with Karen Nelson, the licensed broker in our Short Sale division. She schedules an appointment with each client to discuss their situation and explain their options.

Since Karen is salaried, all of the commission we earn on the short sale is paid to the brokerage. Karen receives a percentage of the profit from short sales in addition to her salary. If our sales agents or competing agents go on an appointment and the clients need a short sale, we pay a 25% referral fee to transfer it to our Short Sale division.

A short sale may not always be in the best interest of your clients. There can often be legal ramifications, income tax consequences, and financial issues that we are not qualified to advise clients about. We advise potential clients, in writing, to speak with an attorney, tax professional, and financial planner to understand the potential consequences of a short sale.

We negotiated a flat-fee deal for our clients with a local attorney. For a $250.00 fee, the clients receive a 45-minute consultation to determine whether they should pursue a short sale. At the end of the process, the same attorney reviews the bank's approval letter to ensure that there are not any hidden liabilities. We earn nothing from referring clients to the attorney other than assurance from an experienced attorney that the short sale is in the client's best interest.

Short sales require many tasks that are not part of a typical real estate transaction. We created a list of the additional tasks we will perform and the associated cost for each. We pay our staff every two weeks so we cannot afford to work for several months on a short sale file without payment, especially since the attorney might tell the client to walk away from the short sale after we have spent months securing a buyer and negotiating with the lien holders.

In order to do what is best for your clients, you must create a business model that does not rely on real estate commissions to be successful. Those who benefit the most from your efforts are the homeowners. As a short sale agent, you must provide weekly updates to the Seller, the title company, the mortgage holder, and the Buyer's agent.

The Sellers will stay in their home longer because of your efforts to secure a short sale. Because a short sale may not be in our Seller's best interests, we might never receive a commission so we need to charge the Seller enough to pay our staff to work for them each week.

Most attorneys require a retainer fee before they begin work on your case. We charge our clients fees to prepare their financial package and a small amount each month *after* our efforts have saved them another monthly payment. Our Short Sale division would not be able to stay open if we did not charge fees for helping the clients submit their short sale package and the monthly fees to continue negotiating on their behalf. Even doctors at free clinics have to earn enough to eat and pay for the medicine they distribute!

I don't like "bait-and-switch" advertising. Therefore, we provide our fee structure to prospective clients before our initial appointment with them. We do not pay our agents any portion of the fees if they fail to tell the client about them in advance. The fees we charge have a lot to do with our success rate. We have a full-time staff dedicated to helping our clients avoid foreclosure.

The people who pay our fees are much more motivated to win. In my experience, these clients provide completed paperwork, keep their home cleaner for potential showings, and respond to phone messages faster. Our short sale Sellers pay on a fee-based system as their short sale progresses through various steps. For us to be able to help them, they must accept our price recommendation and agree to lower the asking price by 5% every two weeks until sold. How many conventional sellers will do *that?*

The most common mistake I see other agents make on short sales is to list the home for the amount the Seller owes and never lower the price. A Loss Mitigator might work on 300 to 400 short sale files at a time. If you send them another file that does not include an offer, they really don't have the time to speak with you, there is nothing to discuss.

Lien holders need *offers* to begin negotiations. A property priced too high does not attract buyers and a property priced too low might look like a "brother-in-law" deal. You should price homes to attract reasonable offers so you can begin negotiations quickly. Failing to lower the asking price could be doing your client a huge disservice!

The price a bank client is willing to accept is usually set based on the average of an appraiser's opinion of value and one or two Broker's Price Opinions (BPO) from local real estate agents. Many appraisers and brokers who complete BPO assignments are very busy and don't pay close attention to defects that may be present on a property.

Thus, whenever possible, you should meet the appraiser and BPO agents sent by the lien holder at the property to ensure that they are aware of defects that may exist. You can point out potential safety and maintenance issues and provide contractor quotes to repair them. You can also provide them with historical data about other comparable properties that have sold. If you don't provide a key safe at the property, anyone who will be establishing the property's value will have to contact you to schedule a time to view the home.

We ask our REO staff to provide an unbiased BPO for the property so that we can submit it to the lien holder. We make sure to reference other unsold homes priced lower than the subject property and call attention to unsold homes with more expensive amenities like swimming pools and three-car garages. We also include a chart showing the percentage of available inventory in our market sold each month to show the Loss Mitigator how long the property will sit on the market if they foreclose on it.

The six major drivers that cause families to sell their home and relocate are marriage, divorce, birth, death, promotion, and transfer. All of these events will continue to occur at the same rate, but in markets like Tucson, where homes fell 40% or more in value since the market peak, many Sellers will owe more than their home is worth and will require a short sale in order to relocate.

Change in Real Life

<u>Loan Modification Success?</u>

A client who lost his job earning $120,000 per year finally found another job after being unemployed more than a year. The new job paid $40,000, one-third of his previous salary. The client's house payment was $2,600 but the gross pay before tax of his new job was $3,333, clearly not enough to make ends meet.

We submitted his package and much to our surprise; the bank lowered the principal balance by $50,000, recast his loan for a new 30-year period, and lowered the interest to a 3% fixed rate! This reduced his payment by over $700.00 per month.

If the homeowner made six payments at the new amount, the bank would make the modification permanent. On the fifth month, our client came back and asked us to sell the home as a short sale. It turns out that a similar home down the street had just sold for $100K less than what our client owed on his home, even after the modification.

Most loan modifications don't address the real problem. Even if banks lower the interest rate to *zero*, most homeowners would still owe far more than the value of their home. Loan modifications will not work until they become *principal* modifications.

23

Telephone Technology

How to use cellular phones, the Internet, e-mail, and toll-free numbers in your business

"It is impossible to transmit speech electrically. The 'telephone' is as mythical as the unicorn."– Johann Christian Poggendorrf

Telephones

Technology has changed the way we manage our lives but there are so many time-saving products available that it's sometimes a challenge to incorporate all of them. Telephones have been utilized for over one hundred years but inventors continually add more features and provide better quality. Telephones utilizing today's technology can connect clients anywhere in the world without using conventional hard-wired phone lines.

Today cellular phones are smaller, lighter, and contain many innovations including high-resolution cameras, video recorders, navigational software, global positioning systems, mapping capabilities, and real-time access to e-mail and the Internet. You can communicate remotely via multiple e-mail accounts and conduct internet searches from anywhere within range of the ever-expanding network of cell phone towers.

Change in Real Life

Stay Connected from Anywhere

We recently went on a vacation to an island off the coast of Belize, Central America. We were surprised to find an internet connection in the home we had rented! Even though I was in a remote part of the world, I could have plugged in a phone and answered every call as if I was in my Arizona office. There were no extra fees or long distance charges, but I'm certain that my wife, Camille, would not have been pleased if I'd have answered the phone!

CHAPTER 23 – TELEPHONE TECHNOLOGY

Agents can carry on a conversation with out-of-state clients throughout the day, send them photos within seconds of taking them, and share face-to-face video conference calls from virtually anywhere using Skype.

We have three offices in Tucson (our main office, a sales office, and our home office) plus remote offices in Pinetop, AZ and Sierra Vista, AZ. In addition to the telephones in each office we have several cell phones, 800 numbers, and fax lines. In total we had more than forty telephones on five separate services that didn't communicate with one another. To enable the systems to communicate we had to pay a third party company to route our calls to each location.

Several friends in my mastermind group (see Chapter 29 on mastermind groups) had switched from "land lines" to Voice-over Internet Protocol (VoIP) phones. Rather than using hard-wired "land lines" or cellular phone towers, these phones use the internet to connect calls. The phones have a USB connection that plugs into any computer and can be used anywhere in the world where internet service is available. The clarity of VoIP phones has vastly improved in recent years. The phones no longer have the tinny sound they once were known to produce.

Switching to a VoIP telephone system enables us to have all of our phones and voicemail on one network. We can easily transfer calls between cell phones, 800 numbers, and all five office locations with the press of a button. The system can handle up to 100 incoming calls at the same time and can seamlessly route calls to where they need to go.

Each location has a local area code so callers won't incur any additional charges to contact you. All phone-related services are one bill and the savings can be as much as $5,000 per year compared to our previous setup. You will experience fewer dropped calls from trying to transfer between systems and more calls can be answered by a person rather than going to voice mail. The $5,000 saved annually is minimal when compared to the $100,000 that could be realized from increased call capture each year!

Voicemail

I typically do not answer calls while I'm in a meeting. Interrupting a meeting to answer the telephone sends a message to the people you're with that the person on the telephone is more important than they are. If I was unable to answer my telephone for a few hours I would usually have at least ten messages waiting in my voicemail.

After finishing a client appointment I would call my voice mail, listen to the recorded messages, and write the caller's name and phone number on a sticky note while driving back to the office. Although I never had an accident, I know that this practice is unsafe and illegal in many areas.

Sometimes new calls would come in while I was listening to the messages that had already been left. I would have to decide whether to hang up to catch the new call or continue listening to the messages and hope that the caller would leave yet another message.

This was a very hectic and disorganized way to conduct business. Over the years I lost many important messages when the sticky note they were written on became stuck to something else or was inadvertently thrown away or misfiled. My desk was a virtual sticky-note forest with dozens of the reminders in varying shapes, sizes, and colors. If a potential client had viewed my work area they might get the impression that I was not very organized.

Change in Real Life

Prune Your Sticky Note Forest

I had acquired hundreds of sticky notes over several years and had stuffed them in a manila folder in my office.

My assistant entered all of the names and contact information on each sticky note into a Microsoft Excel spreadsheet, one note per row. Everything I did not want to lose is now in one location.

It previously could take an hour to rifle through the stack of sticky notes to find the desired information but by using the "Find" command in Microsoft Excel (Ctrl F), I can type the word "plumber" and immediately find all the names of plumbers I had written down on the sticky notes over several years.

The chaos ended when Dave Kipling and Sue Gutierrez, real estate agents in Tucson, showed me www.voicecloud.com. This company transcribes audio voicemails into text and sends the message in an e-mail within one minute of the call. The translation is not always complete and accurate due to callers using slang, speaking incoherently, or referencing the Spanish-named streets in Tucson but you can usually get the gist of the message by reading it.

Each message has an .mp3 file attached so you have the option to listen to the audio version if the text translation is not clear. If you receive the e-mail on a smart phone and need to call the person back, you simply press on the phone number in the message and your cellular telephone will dial the call. There is no longer a need to have your phone in one hand and a pen in the other while driving with your knees! The message is captured and an electronic record is sent to your e-mail.

If you are in a meeting or at a conference and can't take telephone calls you can periodically view the content of your messages to ensure that there isn't an emergency. You can view the message and forward it to someone on your staff within seconds without having to leave the meeting to listen to the message or to speak with anyone about it.

No introduction is usually necessary to forward the message. Just press "Forward," type the first few letters of the person's name you want to receive it, and press "Send." This is a huge time savings for me and our clients receive a response much faster!

With this productivity tool, I can keep my thumb on the pulse of what is happening in our business without becoming personally involved in each situation. A sample message from www.voicecloud.com is provided in Figure 23-1.

Figure 23-1 Voicecloud Message

```
------Original Message------
From: noreply@voicecloud.com
Subject: VoiceCloud Message From: 15203068041
Sent: Jun 16, 2010 8:31 PM

My name is Sergio Xxxxxx I'm calling regarding the house
at 3141 W Casiani please call me back at 520-XXX-XXXX.
I'm interested to get more info on it.
Voice-to-Text by VoiceCloud
```

Managing E-mail

As our business grew, we started receiving more and more e-mails each day. Even though we have trusted employees who have been with us for many years, I still like to know what is going on in all aspects of our business. When the e-mail volume grew to more than 500 per day, I could no longer keep up and began to overlook important e-mails.

My Blackberry cellular telephone can monitor up to ten different e-mail accounts so I created separate e-mail accounts for each of the following categories:

1. Personal – Correspondence with friends and family
2. REO – Tasks and conversations with asset managers

3. Voicemail - Transcribed telephone messages
4. Leads – All inquiries from our advertising
5. HOT! – Emergency e-mail for my staff to reach me. I don't share this address outside our company; otherwise, it would become filled with non-emergency correspondences.

If the e-mail traffic on any account grows too large, I simply split the mail by topic or sender and create a new account to manage the volume. This change has made it much easier for me to view e-mails and find messages quickly. The hot e-mails never exceed more than one or two per day, so I can take the necessary action within seconds of becoming aware of a potential crisis.

800 Numbers

On all of our real estate signs we have the local telephone number of our office and a toll-free 800 number with recorded information about each home. We receive nearly three times more calls from the recorded messages on our 800 numbers than we do on our local telephone numbers. Many homebuyers don't want to speak with a sales person; they just want information about a home.

The 800 numbers allow us to provide buyers with information about the home no matter what time of the day or night they call. We record a separate message for each property so callers can listen to the recorded message by entering the four-digit code associated with the property.

CHAPTER 23 – TELEPHONE TECHNOLOGY

We currently use *three* 800 numbers, one for the homes of conventional sellers, that describes the emotional selling points of their home; one for bank-owned property that explains the process, timeline, and how sales of these homes differ from conventional sales; and one for our Spanish-speaking clients.

When callers dial the 800 numbers, they hear a brief message about our company and then are prompted to enter the four-digit code from the sign or ad that corresponds to the property they called about. After entering the four-digit code they are connected to a recorded message that describes the amenities of the home.

We never say anything on the recording that would disqualify the home for a potential client. This includes providing the number of bedrooms and bathrooms, lot size, square footage, or price. Since most people make emotion-based decisions on where they live, we include information about the awesome sunset views, spacious living areas, relaxing backyards, and cool swimming pools.

At the end of the message, the listener has the option of pressing "zero" to obtain more information. This connects them to our sales office and our trained Inside Sales Associates will determine how to assist them. A majority of the callers just want the price. We always give it to them after asking a series of questions that establish their timing and motivation.

If you have a recorded message that gives callers too many options they'll often hang up before the entire menu had been described. We found that more people leave messages when we make our outgoing message short. Our simple recorded message says, "Thank you for calling Win3 Realty, if you are an agent press 1, if you are not an agent press 2."

Agents calling to ask if a property is still available or about a home they have under contract will be routed to our main office. We have a large staff at that location and a person in the appropriate department will be located to assist the agent.

If the caller presses "2" indicating that they're not an agent, the call is routed to our sales office where their need can be best handled. Non-agent callers who contact us often want to know the price and availability of a certain property. As discussed earlier, our staff provides them the information they request after determining their motivation, timing, and ability

If the caller is not an agent but doesn't want to buy or sell a property they will not fall through the cracks. No matter which selection they make their call will be forwarded by either office to the person best equipped to assist them.

Some clients are routed to me, but if I'm unavailable, either Cristina Candito, our office manager or Stuart Lott, our operations manager will take the call. Both have been trained to determine whether they can assist the client rather than making the caller wait for me to return their call.

Our staff is trained to determine whether my involvement will change the outcome of the situation and whether our relationship with the caller will be harmed if I don't personally take the call (see discussion of TimeTracker™ on p. 37). Many times, a staff member can help the caller faster and better than if I get involved in the situation.

24

High-Tech Tools

Use the Internet, social networking, and
software products to simplify your business

*"Do not follow where the path may lead. Go, instead, where
there is no path and leave a trail."– Ralph Waldo Emerson*

SOLD ON CHANGE!

The Internet has changed real estate sales from local activity to a global activity. We use online advertising that allows people around the world to view our properties. It has become common to correspond with people in other parts of the world daily.

When appropriately integrated into your business, technology can increase your productivity, enabling you to sell substantially more homes in less time. To keep up with the seemingly weekly changes in technology, you'll need to hire a technical support professional.

Whether you hire a tech-savvy employee or contract a company, don't neglect the time-saving opportunities of new technology. You'll need to utilize as many productivity-enhancing products as you can to compensate for the lower commissions being paid on each sale.

Social Networking Sites - Several online search websites enable you to find people who you may have met only briefly. Once a member of these sites, you can leverage your time by typing a single message that can be accessed by everyone you know on Facebook™, Twitter™, LinkedIn™, or other social networking sites.

Electronic Key Safes - The key safes on your listed properties can be electronically monitored. Notifications can be sent to your cell phone so you can receive an alert within minutes of another agent opening the home. This enables you to contact with the agent before they have even finished showing the property to their prospective clients!

HomeFeedback.com™ - We use HomeFeedback.com to automatically request showing feedback from any agent who shows our properties. When agents open the electronic lockbox to obtain the key, an e-mail is automatically sent to them to find out whether their clients liked the home and are thinking of writing an offer on the property.

Our Sellers have 24/7 access to the showing feedback provided by other agents, eliminating the need for them to call me, for me to contact the other agent, and for me to call the client back to tell them what the other agent's clients thought about their home.

ZipForm® - For years I kept a large accordion file in my car that contained a blank copy of every form available from the Arizona Association of Realtors. When I needed a form I would sift through the different compartments of the accordion file to find the appropriate form. On several occasions I discovered that I had not restocked my supply of forms before driving to the client's home.

The ZipForm software provides online access to all of the forms approved by the Arizona Association of Realtors. Because the information is entered on a computer, the chance of it being illegible is greatly reduced. The software highlights each place on the form that requires input so you're much less likely to overlook entering pertinent terms, conditions, or information.

When you fill out the contact information for each client, the software will automatically insert the information on each document utilized throughout the transaction.

DocuSign® - ZipForm software contains a link to DocuSign electronic signature software that enables clients to "sign" documents with the click of a mouse. When we first started using DocuSign in 2006, nearly every agent we sent a contract to called to find out what the strange looking signature was and whether or not it was legal.

A similar stir occurred many years ago when questions were raised over the legality and legitimacy of signatures received via facsimile. Electronic signatures are not new. The ability to use them was signed into law in the 1990s during the Clinton administration.

To use DocuSign you can either convert a document created in ZipForm into a PDF file or scan a paper copy of the contract to create a PDF file. The document that your clients need to sign electronically is then imported into the DocuSign software.

To prepare the contract for your clients, simply scroll to the location that requires their acknowledgement. Paste either a signature line or initial block as appropriate for each client. This is no different from previewing a contract in advance and using a highlighter pen or the "sign here" tabs available at office supply stores at each location that needs to be signed or initialed by your clients.

After setting up a separate DocuSign account for each person who will sign the document, you simply click the "Send" button. A copy of the contract is sent to each client's e-mail. If you're working with a married couple, both spouses will receive a separate e-mail. The clients can access the contract by entering their pre-assigned access code.

The DocuSign software will automatically locate the first place on the contract that requires acknowledgement. The clients can scroll up or down at their own pace to read the contract without feeling pressured for time. If they agree with the contract they simply click their mouse on the initial block or signature line and the appropriate initials or signature will be applied in the signature font style that the client has chosen.

DocuSign automatically scrolls to the next location of the contract that needs to be acknowledged by the client. This process is repeated until all initial blocks, signature lines, and dates have been completed. The "signed" document is then automatically uploaded to the internet so the agent can retrieve it and send it to the other agent and the title company.

If one member of your clients' household has already relocated to another city, a counter offer received from a Seller would typically be faxed (1) to the Buyer's agent, and then faxed (2) to the Buyer who would sign it and fax it (3) back to the agent. The contract would be sent via fax (4) to Mrs. Buyer who would print it, sign it and fax it (5) back to the agent. The agent would then fax (6) the signed document to the Seller's agent and the title company.

Each time a document is sent via fax it is converted into a series of zeros and ones and then reassembled upon arrival at the receiving fax machine. Often the document is not reassembled exactly the way it was sent and there is a visible shift in the data giving it a jagged appearance. These *transcription lines* become more evident each time a document is faxed.

After being faxed six times, there is a good chance the document could be so distorted it would become very difficult to read. With DocuSign the contract will be received in both locations at once and the signatures will be consolidated on one page without any degradation in quality caused by faxing multiple times.

DocuSign also provides your clients with an electronic copy of everything that they've signed so you don't have to worry about providing paper copies for their records. This product will save enough time and gas to pay for itself very quickly. Many times we'll have signed documents back in our office in less time than it would take to drive one way to meet with the client.

Before using DocuSign, I purchased a fax machine for many of our clients who lived a long distance from my office. The money I saved in time and gasoline was well worth the cost of the $100 fax machines, but that is no longer necessary with DocuSign.

25

Capturing Clients

Using SalesJunction® to track conversion, schedule follow-up, and control call volume

"Success is the ability to go from one failure to another with no loss of enthusiasm."– Winston Churchill

When your advertising begins to work, you'll need to purchase customer relationship management software to track and communicate with all of the people who've contacted you about their housing needs. We have used both Agent Office® and Top Producer® but neither provided what we needed.

In my opinion, Agent Office has not done a good job of keeping up with technology. The program still has the look and feel of the MS-DOS operating system from the 1980s. Top Producer has a cleaner new look, and an awesome automated market comparison, but is not designed to support a team like ours. Although multiple people can access the data, there's not a way to hide one agent's appointments or personal clients from the other agents on your team.

We researched many of programs available and decided on a product called SalesJunction®. We made our decision because the program was totally scalable, intuitive, easy to use, and inexpensive. If your business changes and you need to be able to track new data parameters, SalesJunction allows you to create a new field for the data in less than a minute. When we needed another column in Agent Office, their technical support representative told us, "Just use the 'Birthday' column."

SalesJunction allows you to set permissions for each user that establishes the content that they can access. This ensures that one agent will not have access another agent's clients. Your existing customer database from Agent Office or Top Producer can easily be imported into Sales Junction.

CHAPTER 25 – CAPTURING CLIENTS

Like Agent Office and Top Producer, the program will automatically send reminder messages to your staff or scheduled e-mails to clients who are not yet ready to act. The software will also send automated e-mails to remind you to follow up with those who have already bought or sold a home with you.

The cost of SalesJunction is only $100 per user per year, which is very inexpensive compared to other products. The system is hosted online so you won't have to purchase a separate server or grant a vendor access to your company's computer system. You can access the system from any available Internet connection, even from your cellular phone.

If you need to know what's going on in your business, this is the program to use! We started using SalesJunction in April 2009. We started with a clean slate and began building the program as we went along. The technical support personnel have been awesome to work with. They've added several features and reports to the program to help meet our needs. We've been able to seamlessly transfer data from Top Producer, Agent Office, and Microsoft Outlook.

We embedded our buyer and seller scripts into the software so our Inside Sales staff can reference it without looking away from their computer screen. We've arranged the data fields in the program to follow the order that questions are asked in the script. All client information can be entered while our staff is on the telephone with the prospective client so it doesn't take any additional time to input data after the telephone call has ended.

We tracked 14,000 telephone calls over an eighteen-month period and can tell you the hours of the day when the most calls come into our office. Having this information will enable you to schedule your staff to work during peak call times. We can also accurately forecast which months will be slow or busy so we know when to increase or decrease our advertising.

We track the effectiveness of our team by regularly checking how many telephone calls were made by each staff member, the average length of each call, the number of appointments that were set, how many appointments were held, and how many clients ended up buying or selling a home with us.

Because it's so important to call prospective clients back quickly, we track the time it takes to return each call from the time we were initially contacted. We review this information weekly to ensure that we're adequately staffed and to ensure that someone isn't burning through a bunch of leads but not setting any appointments.

Besides tracking the conversion ratio of our Inside Sales staff, we also track the conversion of our Outside Sales agents. We know how many appointments with Buyers or Sellers they take each week, how many each agent converts to listing agreements or Buyer/Broker agreements, and most importantly how many they close. This helps us determine which agent to book on appointments. We are not paid unless clients act, so we want to assign the agent who is the best fit for each client's personality and has the skill set to help them.

CHAPTER 25 – CAPTURING CLIENTS

Regularly tracking the effectiveness of each team member will enable you to spot problems early and take corrective action before it's too late. Every two weeks we check the performance of each staff member to ensure that they're winning and the company is winning.

If the staff member isn't earning enough to live comfortably, we'll intervene to find out what's holding them back. Sometimes simply changing a word or two in their presentation can make a huge difference in their effectiveness. If you wait until an employee quits, it's usually too late to get them back and help them achieve success.

SalesJunction provides a calendar for agents to track their appointments. We teach our agents that soccer games, school plays, PTA meetings, church commitments, and date nights with their spouse are all "appointments" that need to be kept. We encourage our agents to block time for these family activities.

Our Inside Sales Manager has a master calendar that shows the availability for each agent. If a prospective client requests a specific time, she can quickly determine who is available and which agent's personality and expertise would best match the person on the telephone.

The SalesJunction administrator (a designated staff person in your office) can view the calendar and log-in history for all users. If an agent has not updated their SalesJunction account for several days, we assume that they're busy. We do not assign any more appointments to them until they are caught up.

If a potential client doesn't opt to use our company, we review the client notes to determine whether the Inside Sales staff felt the prospect was motivated. If there is a mismatch between the outcome reported by the Outside Sales agent and the notes from the Inside Sales staff, we make an "autopsy" call to the prospect in an attempt to find out why the client did not choose to use our company.

We have found instances when clients are more comfortable working with a woman rather than a man or perhaps with an agent fluent in their native language. We always try to accommodate the prospective clients. On several occasions we have been able to schedule another appointment and win their business the second time around.

Because we track where every lead originated, we know the advertising mechanism that caused each client to contact us. This knowledge enables us to do more of what works and less of what doesn't work. For every type of advertising we do, we have developed an expectation of the results we will produce each time we run the campaign.

For example, when the number of inquiries slows down on short sales, we increase our short sale advertising until the call volume returns to normal. When we get more calls than we can handle, we shut off the advertising until we're caught up. Unlike most real estate businesses, ours is *very* controllable!

26

Advertising Advice
Using non-conventional advertising to give Buyers and Sellers what they are looking for

"Don't judge each day by the harvest you reap but by the seeds that you plant." – Robert Louis Stevenson

We utilize technology in our advertising to increase the visibility of our client's properties. You can create a separate website for each property you list and utilize the syndicated advertising agreements negotiated by your MLS. When we list a property for sale locally it's also listed for sale on the following national websites:

AOL.com/Real Estate,
Backpage.com
CLRSearch.com
Cyberhomes.com
Enormo.com
ERealInvestor.com
Fizber.com
FrontDoor.com
Google.com
Homefinder.com
Hotpads.com
LakeHomesUSA.com
LandWatch.com
Lycos.com
Local.com
Military.com

MyRealty.com
OceanHomesUSA.com
Oodle.com
OpenHouse.com
Overstock.com
PropBot.com
Realtor.com
ResortScape.com
RiverHomesUSA.com
SecondSpace.com
Trulia.com
Vast.com
Walmart.com
Yahoo.com/Real Estate
Zillow.com

Between 2006 and 2009 an average of 12.5% of the properties on the Tucson MLS were sold each month. During the same time we have had 30% to 42% of our listed properties under contract. I am confident that the reason there is such a difference between the MLS average and our company's results is the wide exposure we provide and the methods we use to market our properties.

CHAPTER 26 – ADVERTISING ADVICE

Besides "for sale" signs and exposure on real estate sites on the Internet, we also use Craigslist and Google ads to attract buyers. Google has conducted a huge amount of research to find the words that are searched most frequently on the Internet. By providing Google with a daily budget you can pay to make your website come up at the top of most searches.

After selling the home they live in, most sellers intend to buy another home. For this reason, we market to sellers as if they were buyers. We employ technology that will provide a 24/7 automated search of properties within minutes of the prospect asking for the information.

Available homes are displayed on a satellite map of the area so prospects can see the homes currently for sale or recently sold. By moving their computer's mouse over each sold or active home, they can view the address, price, square footage, and several photos of the property. We give users free access to our search site to demonstrate its value before asking them for their contact information. The agents who make it easiest for potential clients to obtain information will gain the largest share of the market and earn the most money.

Advertising Mistakes

Many real estate agents do not know how to advertise themselves or their business effectively. New agents seem to observe what other agents are doing and copy them without bothering to find out how well the advertising works. The most common mistake I observe is agents using half of their business card for an outdated glamour shot of themselves.

SOLD ON CHANGE!

In my experience, most clients don't care what company you work for or what you looked like in high school. I'm not trying to offend anyone but the buyer of a home doesn't care whether you have a gold jacket, a well-known rock, or a balloon (unless you'll give them a ride). Do doctors, attorneys, accountants or other professionals need gimmicks or photos of themselves to attract business? Why do so many real estate agents believe that these things matter?

When traveling, I always make a point to pick up local real estate magazines. Besides finding huge photos of the agent and oversized company logos on nearly every page, I have come to expect at least one kook dressed in a batman suit or as some other fairy tale, comic book, or cartoon character.

I also expect to find at least one agent who has thought up some clever line that incorporates either their first or last name in their slogan like, "When you need to sell, call Nell." Neither of these approaches is effective at building business. Brand recognition maybe, but not *business*. Would consumers really trust a person in a superhero costume with the most important financial decision of their lives?

Besides gimmicks, clever slogans, outdated photos, and oversized company logos, the biggest mistake I see agents make is in the *content* of their ads. Most ads crowd 9 to 15 homes per page, depending upon how much of the space the agent used to promote themselves or their company.

The tiny ads for each home usually contain a thumbnail photo of the home and two or three lines of text. Most agents include specific data such as the number of bedrooms, bathrooms, and square footage. This sounds logical, but in fact, each number could give the potential buyer a reason to *disqualify* the home from consideration.

A 100-page magazine with an average of 12 homes per page would offer 1200 possibilities for potential buyers. The odds are slim that a buyer who is ready to act will thumb through the pages of the magazine, see the tiny photo of a home, and say, "That's the one for me!" If shoe stores used this method to advertise each of their products specifically, they would hang a banner on the side of their building that read, **"FOR SALE: Brown, Size 10½, EEE, penny loafers with tassels $59.99."**

How many people would this type of advertising attract to the store? Don't you think more people might respond to a sign that simply read, "Big Sale Today"?

Most agents spend their entire advertising budget on the grocery store magazines because their clients *expect* them to. Just because your competitors waste their money on ineffective advertising does not mean that you should too.

When our prospective clients ask which magazines I plan to use to advertise their home I simply say, "None". Those ads don't work as effectively as my advertising and I can prove it! I give the client a copy of the agent ranking report from our MLS and ask them to find agents in the top fifty who advertise in all the magazines.

It usually takes the Sellers quite a while to find even one agent from the magazines. When they finally find an agent, I ask them to compare the buyer-side transactions of the agent who advertises in the magazine to the number of buyers we have attracted and closed. Then I ask them, "If these ads worked don't you think all the agents in the magazine would be in the top fifty?"

I have saved thousands of dollars by not running these worthless ads. The question cuts straight to the point and helps removes the Seller's expectation that their home will appear in the grocery store magazines.

When *buying* real estate, the three most important rules might be location, location, location, but the three most important rules of *selling* real estate are:

1. Buyers want houses
2. Sellers want Buyers
3. Nothing else matters

Your advertising should inform potential clients that you have the *homes* that buyers want and the *buyers* that sellers want. In my experience, nothing has proven to be more effective.

Using these simple principles, our small, largely unknown company has increased sales in the Tucson market every year since opening in 2004. At first, we experienced only small gains but over the past three years, we've added two hundred more sales each year to the previous year's total.

CHAPTER 26 – ADVERTISING ADVICE

Without running a single ad in the grocery store magazines, our advertising caused more than 8,000 buyers to contact us in 2009. That is an average of nearly one buyer *every hour* all year long! Having the most buyers automatically attracts the most sellers because sellers need buyers.

This is how to do it:
1) Advertise to attract more people than you can service
2) Determine the timing and motivation of each caller
3) Fire clients who are rude or difficult to work with
4) Incubate those who are not ready to act
5) Sell to those who are ready now

27

Soliciting to your Sphere

How to get the people you know to tell the people they know about your business

"The best helping hand that you will ever receive is the one at the end of your own arm."– Fred Dehner

Most agents do not do a very good job of using the people around them to market themselves. Everyone sees or communicates with other people on a regular basis. Through regular contact, you may have the ability to influence some of the decisions of the people in your personal *sphere of influence.*

Let's assume that you know 200 people and each of those people knows 200 people. It you educate the people you know about your business niche, and they tell the people that they know, you could potentially influence the decisions of 40,000 people. Figure 27-1 contains an exercise to help quantify the people in your "sphere of influence."

You cannot automatically expect all of the people you know to tell all of the people they know that you are a real restate agent. Aside from your parents and your spouse, few people will convey a message about your business to their friends unless you give them a *reason.*

Do you possess a unique skill or ability related to real estate? Do you know of available properties that other agents do not know are for sale? Is there a recent success story that would warm the hearts of others to make them want to use your services? Your friends would pass these types of things along to their friends if you educated them.

When new agents join our company we ask them to make a list of all of the people in their "sphere of influence" so our marketing department can inform them of the agent's decision to join our company.

CHAPTER 27 – SOLICITING TO YOUR SPHERE

Figure 27-1 Sphere of Influence

YOUR SPHERE OF INFLUENCE

Your sphere of influence consists of all the people you've come into contact with at some point in your life. Each of these people has their own sphere of influence. If all of the people you know start telling all of the people they know about your business, the list of potential clients would be 800 pages long! People in your sphere could include:

FAMILY
Spouse's family
Parents
Grandparents
Aunts & uncles
Brothers, sisters, cousins
Nieces, nephews, children

FRIENDS
Childhood friends
Neighbors
Roommates

PROFESSIONAL
Doctors
Dentists
Accountants
Attorneys
Architects
Home Builders
Mechanics
*Anyone whose services you purchase

SCHOOL
Teachers
Classmates
Coaches
Teammates
Fraternity/Sorority siblings

FORMER JOBS
Bosses
Co-workers
Subordinates
Contractors
Salespersons
Maintenance persons

CHURCH
Pastors
Office Staff
Bible study group

CLUBS & ORGANIZATIONS
Troop leaders
Scouts
Language clubs
Hobby clubs
Professional associations
Charitable institutions

STRANGERS
Waiting rooms
Adjacent airplane passengers
Real Estate magazine readers
Diners in restaurants

On a notepad, write all of the names that come to mind related to each of the categories above. When you've exhausted your memory on one category, move to the next and repeat the process until you've completed a separate sheet for each of the eight categories.

SOLD ON CHANGE!

A sample of the introductory letter we send is provided in below in Figure 27-2. We advertise for our agents because we know they will become busy and fail to do it for themselves.

Figure 27-2 Introductory Letter

Hi Jerry!

It's Annie Agent! - Your Tucson Real Estate Professional. I'm writing to let you know that **I've joined The Win3 Realty Team!**

As you know, the real estate industry is experiencing many changes. I have made this exciting move in order to improve the level of service that I can provide for you! Win3 Realty is a full service real estate agency with a unique team system and performance guarantees that ensure your success whether you are buying or selling a home.

Win3 Realty has stayed ahead of the changing market by securing the best deals for our clients including bank foreclosures, short sales and other distressed properties. By working with me, you will have exclusive access to properties on the day the properties are listed, before other buyers even know they are for sale! I can help you locate ALL the properties that are for sale in Tucson, not just those listed on the MLS.

The Win3 Realty Team offers experience and knowledge that will help you meet your goals and achieve your dreams. Even though the average REALTOR® in Tucson sold only two properties in 2009, our team closed over 500 transactions! We found homes for nearly 150 buyers and were the #1 selling team in Tucson for the second consecutive year.

I am excited to be part of The Win3 Realty Team and I look forward to continuing to provide you with winning solutions and professional results. If you know of anyone needing to buy or sell a home, please contact me or have them give me a call!

Warm Regards,

Annie Agent
The Win3 Realty Team

When we sent this letter to the sphere of influence of one new agent, she received an immediate response from a past client who owned several properties in Tucson. He said, "I didn't know you knew how to do short sales" and proceeded to list *ten* properties with her! How much potential business do you have that isn't being captured?

We also send a monthly newsletter to inform clients of market changes, share success stories, and provide information on recently passed legislation that will affect real estate sales. We send all communications with the agent's name and contact information rather than that of the office.

We strive to be known as the company that knows what is happening in the market. A home is the largest investment most people make so they naturally have an interest in whether home prices are rising or falling. Rather than providing our clients with irrelevant information, such as recipes or magnetic calendars, we prefer to be providers of critical and timely market data. We show potential clients that we know the market and can help them accomplish their goals. A sample of our monthly newsletter is below.

Dear Clients,

During the past three years, Tucson has been in a declining real estate market where buyers have been waiting for prices to stabilize and sellers have been waiting for them to increase. The chart below illustrates that both of these things have begun to occur, so be prepared for the market to rebound during the coming months.

It's easy to recognize the winter lows and the summer highs on the chart below. Since Arizona doesn't participate in Daylight Savings Time, in the winter it's dark by the time most people get off work but in the

summer it is light enough to show homes until 9:00 in
the evening. Most families wait for the summer school
break to make their move, which adds to the cyclical
nature of our real estate market. In Tucson, we sell
nearly twice as many homes in June as we do in January.

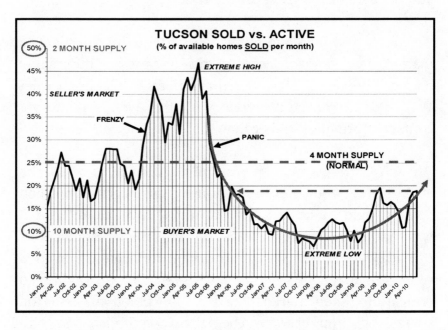

In 2002 and 2003 (prior to the "investor invasion") we
sold 16% to 17% of the MLS inventory in January and then
worked our way up to 27% to 28% in the summer months. In
2004, Tucson was named by Money magazine as one of the
top 20 appreciating markets in the country and during
the next two years, out-of-state investors came in
droves to purchase Tucson real estate. During the
slowest month in 2004, almost 30% of available inventory
was sold and at the market peak in June 2005, more than
47% of the MLS inventory was sold in one month!

January is always the slowest month of the year for real
estate sales because the offers are written in December,
the darkest and most hectic time of the year. Typically,
only 6% to 8% of MLS inventory sells in January but in
2010, January sales were higher than they've been in the
past three years. Market activity usually increases as

CHAPTER 27 – SOLICITING TO YOUR SPHERE

the days get longer and we approach the summer selling season.

At Win3 Realty, we specialize in market research. We can give you in-depth information about any area. We do our homework and offer creative programs to help our clients achieve their dreams. Even in this slow economy there are Tucson neighborhoods in high demand with more than 25% of the listed properties being sold each month.

There are also low demand areas with only 3% of the properties selling each month. Do you think it's important to know this before you decide to buy or sell? Call me to find out what the market is doing in your neighborhood. You might be surprised! Let's schedule an appointment to determine what's best for you.

WHY YOU SHOULD BUY NOW:
The market has created a "Perfect Storm" for buyers
- Interest rates are near record lows
- Prices in some neighborhoods are on the rise
- The income tax credit has been extended beyond first-time home buyers

More than three trillion dollars (that's TWELVE zeros!) were printed last year which will diminish the value of existing dollars and cause high inflation. Because the dollars are worth less, the countries who buy our bonds (China) will require a higher rate of interest, which will cause rates on loans to increase accordingly. A higher cost of money causes the price of everything to increase, including real estate. **ACT NOW!**

WHY YOU SHOULD SELL NOW:
Most sellers are also buyers because when they sell one home, they usually buy another.

- You'll be able to take advantage of the buyer benefits listed above on your new purchase
- MLS inventory is very low and we're receiving multiple offers on many of our listed properties

SOLD ON CHANGE!

- As interest rates and prices increase, it will be harder for buyers to qualify for a loan to buy your home
- We offer a *Home Swap* program for sellers that will save you money when selling one home and moving into a larger one. The savings can enable you to net more money at closing than the buyers pay for your home!

If your $200,000 home has fallen in value by 25%, it is now worth $150,000. You may not be willing or able to absorb a $50,000 loss but if you are buying a $300,000 home, that Seller has lost $75,000 in value so you would actually profit $25,000 by moving! As the price of your home increases, so will the price of the home you are planning to buy. **ACT NOW!**

In 2009, Win3 Realty brought 144 buyers to the closing table, twice as many as any other agent or team in Tucson! Our unconventional advertising attracts more than 200 buyer inquiries per week and we have 14,000 clients in our database who are not yet ready to act. That's twice as many buyers as there are listed properties in the entire MLS!

We're certain that we can find a buyer for your home, so give us a call. We'll tell you the truth about your property's value in today's market. Whether you are buying or selling, now is the time to act. Give us a call and ***Start Packing!***

28

Requesting Referrals

Using home tours and client appreciation events to attract people to your business

"A wise man will make more opportunities than he finds."
– Francis Bacon

Guided Home Tours, Not Open Houses

Craig Proctor taught us that home tours were a much better use of our time than sitting at an open house for several hours waiting for a few people stop by. We have been running guided group tours one or two Saturdays per month since 2006. We advertise the tour via e-mail to our past clients and to buyers in our database who are not yet ready to purchase.

A tour is a good way for potential buyers to see different parts of the city and to understand the amenities that are included at different price points. The group setting allows prospective clients to see multiple homes without feeling pressured to buy any of them. Tours are a great way to leverage your time. Typically between fifteen and thirty people show up for the tours on Saturday mornings. We sometimes accomplish the equivalent of 240 showings in *three hours* by showing eight properties to thirty buyers at once!

Have you ever seen 20 or 30 people all looking at the same home at the same time? We meet-at our office or a coffee shop near the first home on the tour. We form a caravan and when we drive up to each property on the tour, it looks like a funeral procession. All of the neighbors up and down the street come outside to see what is going on!

We've had Sellers whose homes are listed with other companies cross the street to ask us for a business card. They tell us that we've brought more people to their neighbor's home in five minutes than they've had visit their house in the past six months!

CHAPTER 28 – REQUESTING REFERRALS

Our tours usually include stops at eight properties that are the best deals on the market. Sometimes the tours don't include any of our listed properties. We ask the agents running the tours to find the best deals in the city so our tour remains credible. If you only show your own listed properties, people will stop showing up.

We start the tour by having everyone sign a Buyer/Broker agreement to ensure that we're compensated for the research and effort spent to conduct the tour. Before leaving to view properties, we give a recap of the properties featured on our previous tour. Often times, six of the eight properties that we viewed on the previous tour are under contract by the next tour. That says a lot for the properties we select because only 6% to 18% of the MLS has been sold in any month over the past three years!

One agent usually leads the tour and another stays behind to lock up the property and answer questions for stragglers, as these are usually the serious buyers. If the agents sell a home on the tour, it's treated as a sphere lead and the agents conducting the tour split the commission and the associated work between them.

The tour photos are great for getting new property listings and they can also be used as an incentive for price reductions by telling a client, "We have a tour coming up in your neighborhood on Saturday and if we can get your home priced right we'll include it on our tour, but only if it's seen as a good deal by the buyers!"

SOLD ON CHANGE!

A sample e-mail invitation for our home tour is provided in Figure 28-1.

Figure 28-1 Home Tour E-mail Invitation

NORTHWEST HOME TOUR
The BEST Deals on the Market!

April 10th, 2010

Please join us this Saturday for the
Win3 Realty Northwest Tour of Homes!

When: Sat. 4/10 from 9:00 am to 12 noon

Where: Starbucks on the SW Corner of Oracle/Ina
  Meet promptly at 8:45AM (tour leaves at 9:00 AM)

RSVP: tour@win3realty.com

Check Out Why Win3 Realty is Selling So Many Homes!
We will tour FORECLOSURES, SHORT SALES and OTHER
GREAT DEALS currently on the market in NW Tucson!

Information about the properties featured
on the tour will not be provided in advance.
Come prepared to shop, buy and have fun!

We'll see you this Saturday!

Asking for Referrals

Buying a home is a process, not an event. It usually takes at least three months or more from a prospect's initial contact to signing the papers and obtaining the keys. Many real estate agents wait until the last day of the three-month process to ask for referrals from their clients.

This is far too late in the process because much of the excitement has dissipated. Many external forces can influence how smoothly the closing goes. In my experience, the best time to ask a client for a referral is when the contract is first accepted and signed. With either buyers or sellers, this is when their euphoria is at its highest.

Have you ever purchased a new car and then on the drive home from the dealership noticed all of the cars on the road that are just like yours? There were probably just as many cars of that make and model on the road during your drive to the dealership but you didn't notice them. Immediately after making your purchase you have a heightened awareness of the other cars like yours, but after a few weeks you won't notice them anymore.

Homebuyers and sellers experience the same "high" for a brief time after receiving an accepted offer on a home. For a few weeks, they will have a heightened awareness of other homebuyers and sellers who are making a similar decision. They will overhear other consumers discussing their experiences and will often interject to share their research and excitement.

The time to ask for a referral is when your client's level of excitement is at its highest. Ask them to tell everyone they know how quickly you were able to help them buy or sell their home before issues beyond your control can affect your client's willingness to recommend you.

If a lender fails to get the documents processed in a timely manner, your client will have to reschedule their moving company and all of the friends they had lined up to help them move. Even though the delay is not due to anything that you did, your client will be stressed and possibly angry with you! This is not the time to ask them for a referral!

If you had asked the client for referrals at the beginning of their home-buying process instead of waiting for the transaction to close, you could already be working with several of their friends and family members before the lender made them angry.

After the sale, it's a good idea to stay in communication with your clients periodically. Because real estate is such a large portion of the average person's net worth, most clients appreciate knowing how the local market is performing and the prices at which other homes in their area are selling. This keeps you at the top of your client's mind in case other people they know are contemplating a move.

Client Appreciation

We have an annual customer appreciation party to reward the people who have put their trust in our business. We tried having the party at the end of the year but December is a very hectic time of the year for most people with holiday parties, gift shopping and out of town guests.

We opted to have our client event each year in October, before the holiday season starts, but after the intense heat of the Tucson summer has passed. Since 2005, we've hosted an

Oktoberfest celebration for our clients at our home. The attendance has grown to well over 100 clients each year. We serve authentic German food and everyone seems to enjoy visiting with one another, especially our investors.

Figure 28-2 Client Testimonial Invitation

We've helped nearly 2,000 clients successfully buy or sell their homes so we ask them to tell others about their experience with our company. Instead of us telling the 14,000 people in our database what we will do for them, I thought it would be much better to videotape our clients telling everyone what we have *done*.

We chose a movie theme for this special event and invited our clients to be the "stars" in our movie. We treated the clients to a steak dinner at the nicest steakhouse in Tucson if they went on camera to give a testimonial about their experience with our company. The invitation for this client testimonial event is provided in Figure 28-2.

We hired a video production company to provide lighting and professional recording equipment. We set up a miniature set in a private room at the restaurant and recorded each individual or couple as they arrived at the event. Seventy-two of our past clients went on camera to tell others about their experience with our company. We'd prepared a list of eleven questions to ask each individual or couple and provided the list of questions to our clients before they went on camera.

The steakhouse party was a huge success! I had no idea that so many of our client's could recite our company philosophy of always putting them first. The videos could not have been better if they were scripted! Our clients said some very nice things about our company and actors could not duplicate their sincerity. A list of the questions we asked on camera is provided in Figure 28-3.

Figure 28-3 Video Testimonial Questions

Questions for Video Testimonials

1) How did you hear about Win3 Realty?

2) What was it that led you to work with Win3 Realty?

3) Describe your experience with <u>other</u> <u>agents</u> before you hired Win3 Realty...

4) Describe your experience working with Win3 Realty...

5) Was there a specific Win3 Realty program that worked for you? Please share your success story of how it helped you...

6) In your experience, how does Win3 Realty compare to other real estate companies you've worked with?

7) Describe your experience working with our <u>team</u> <u>system</u>...

8) Would you recommend Win3 Realty to your family and friends?

9) Please comment about how your Win3 Realty <u>agent</u> met or exceeded your expectations and kept their promises to you...

10) What did you like best about your Win3 Realty <u>agent</u>?

11) Is there anything else that you'd like to add?

THANK YOU!!!

Buying or selling a home is an emotional experience and the smiles and satisfaction really came through on the video, especially from the clients who had successfully gone through a short sale with us. After editing out the interviewer's questions, we had an hour of footage from the raving fans of our company.

We grouped the responses to each of the eleven questions together so that each question was followed by the response from everyone who attended. We also split the video into *thirty-four* mini-videos to be sent periodically to prospective clients who are not yet ready to act.

Each video is less than two minutes in length and contains three or four brief testimonials from our clients. We can also loop the entire video in our office for prospective clients to watch if they arrive early for their appointment.

Ask past clients to help promote your business. It's well worth the cost of a meal because their endorsement will encourage others to buy and sell their home with you. Now when we contact potential clients, our past clients do the selling for us!

Other Marketing Ideas

Install Signs Early - Unless specifically told not to do so, we install a Win3 Realty sign at vacant properties on the day we get the listing. We place a "Coming Soon" rider on the sign for properties not yet listed to stimulate more interest (everyone wants what they can't have).

For example, we currently have over 300 signs in the ground and average more than 200 sign calls each week. If on average it takes three weeks to complete pre-marketing activities before a property goes active on the MLS, we expect to generate two extra buyer calls per property by installing the signs as soon as the property is assigned to us by the bank.

Two additional calls may not sound like a lot, but since we expect to sell over 500 listed properties per year, putting the signs up early will create 1,000 more buyer calls than if we hadn't done so. If we close only 5% of the buyers who contact us, we will have 50 more buyer-side closings per year just from the calls generated by the "Coming Soon" riders!

Preferred Lender Flyers - We have found that most buyers, especially first-time buyers don't care which lending company they use, they just want the lowest interest rate. Buyers' agents often try to convince their clients to use their lending partner and some agents become angry when the Seller requires them to get a loan qualification letter from a different lender.

We place flyers in the homes for the lender that our Seller requires to pre-qualify the buyers. Several of the Seller-endorsed lenders offer a free appraisal and credit report if the buyers obtain their loan through their company. Because we are getting the information into the Buyer's hands, the flyers have reduced the number of complaints from other agents and have produced more loans for the Seller's preferred lenders.

Buy Used Key Safes - Every time we get low on Supra® electronic key boxes, we send an e-flyer with a "Wanted" poster to every agent in our market. The response has been great every time we run the ad!

SOLD ON CHANGE!

We pay $60 for used key safes in good condition and $80 if the key safes are brand new. New key safes cost over $100 apiece, but we've saved over $7,000 by purchasing the key safes from other agents leaving the business. We've even hired an agent to work at our company who was initially attracted by our offer to buy key safes.

29

Mastermind Membership

Why to join or create a mastermind group and how to hold its members accountable

"All who would win joy must share it; happiness was born a twin."– Lord Byron

Sharing in a Mastermind Group

Many experiments have been conducted to demonstrate the creative power of the human brain. When a task is given to a group of people with no instructions of how to perform the task, each person will go about accomplishing it differently. If you review the method that each person used to accomplish the task and then adapt the best portion of each person's process, you would have the most efficient and effective way to perform the task.

A group of people in the same profession can learn a lot from one another. Everyone who sells real estate is doing *something* to attract, convert, and sell to clients. How many clients you could attract if you had a copy of the best ad each agent in your group developed? If everyone in the group contributed an electronic copy of their best ad, you could quickly replace their name and contact information with yours and in a matter of minutes you would have several ads that have been proven to produce qualified leads.

I'm a member of several real estate chat groups where agents share with one another. The idea is to share marketing ideas or new productivity tools you find with other members of the group. Just think how much your business could be improved if every day hundreds of agents shared what was working best for them. Unfortunately most people take much more from these groups than they give. It takes time to share, but I try to set an example for others in the group by sharing as much as possible.

CHAPTER 29 –MASTERMIND MEMBERSHIP

I don't know why more real estate agents do not create or join mastermind groups. By regularly attending national conferences and training events, I've met hundreds of agents from all over the United States and Canada. Most of the people I meet have a similar mindset to mine. Since we are all willing to invest time and money to educate ourselves, why not share and learn from one another too?

It's scary to spend money on advertising when your income is falling, but if you don't change what you do, your results won't change! You can benefit greatly by surrounding yourself with other business owners who are making similar changes rather that waiting for the market to change.

Over the past few years, I've developed close friendships with agents in other cities who are life-long learners like me. We share our thoughts and notes from meetings and conferences as well as e-mail notifications we receive from vendors trying to sell a new product. We keep each other informed about what is working or not working well in our business.

We alert others in our group to changes we experience in our markets to determine whether the change is local or national in scope. When I recently noticed a 65% reduction in offers from one month to the next I sent a quick e-mail to my mastermind group to see if anyone else was experiencing a similar trend. Within a few minutes, we had data points from all over the country and verified our hypothesis that the slowdown was due to the expiration of the federal tax credit.

Take the time to get to know other agents both in and out of your market area. Many agents won't share with others in their local market because they have the perception that if they share with a competitor there will be less business for them. Although there may be a few things that should not be shared locally, there will always be plenty of business for those who stay ahead of change and strive to improve their business.

I teach accredited short sale classes at Hogan School of Real Estate in Tucson to help local agents become more successful at attracting and closing short sales. I provide a lot of useful information, and students repeatedly ask why I am training my competitors. I remind the student that it takes two real estate agents to close every deal. If I can help them become more successful, it will make my job easier, more homes will sell, and prices and commissions will stop falling.

I've been involved in several national mastermind groups through Craig Proctor's Quantum Leap coaching program, REObroker.com, and the National REO Broker's Association. I've also established a local mastermind group with other agents in our market. It was a little uncomfortable at first, but we have since become good friends. After getting to know one another, we have learned, shared, and had a lot of fun at monthly dinners with two other agent couples in Tucson.

We have shared ads to attract employees, the names of promising job applicants that we were unable to hire, technology to become more productive, and documents that educate other agents about the needs of our bank clients. We never talk about price, commission, or client information. The two other couples in our group attended and financially supported the Make-A-Wish fundraiser we held on my 50th birthday and I've met them at several conferences and have introduced them to others I know in the industry.

Reach out to other agents in your local market. If you've completed a transaction with someone and admired the way they operate, invite them to dinner. It may feel awkward at first but sharing something that they can use will break the ice and usually they will be inclined to share something back with you. You never know where the friendship could lead.

Create Your Own Mastermind Group

A mastermind group should consist of like-minded, creative friends who freely bounce innovative concepts off one another and build on each other's ideas. In order for the group to function as a "think tank," all members must commit to taking the time to share what is working best for them with others in the group. The goal of each member should be to improve the profitability of their business and help each member do the same with theirs.

All members should be peers with a similar income, business volume, and entrepreneurial innovation to be of value to the group. When a group is diluted with members who are not at the same level, low-producing members will not be able to share or further the group's education. You should join a group consisting of business owners at your same level of business and move to a higher-level group when your business increases in volume.

The optimum size of a group varies by how technical the tasks might be, but I've found that groups of three to twelve people are the most effective. To protect its synergy, the group should be very exclusive with membership of qualified agents by invitation only. Only those members approved by 75% or more of the existing members should be allowed to join.

The number of active members should be capped at no more than twenty-five members. Face-to-face meetings should be held at least twice per year in cities where a member of the group resides. The member in the host city should be responsible for procuring a meeting room and arranging a tour of their office so that the group members can meet key members of the host's team.

Members who do not share regularly should be expelled from the group. If only a few people take the time to share, the good sharers will become frustrated with those who don't reciprocate. They will stop sharing and the benefit of the group will be lost. The group should disband if membership and participation decreases substantially or when the educational value is no longer worth the time and expense to attend the meetings.

30

Succeed
By Sharing

How sharing time, talent, and financial resources can help you achieve success

"The more credit you give away, the more will come back to you. The more you help others, the more they will want to help you."– Brian Tracy

SOLD ON CHANGE!

Save For Your Dreams

People often ask me why I share with others. I guess I hadn't thought about it much; it's just something my parents always did and that I want to do. My wife feels the same way. My mother was in charge of our family's finances. Before any of my five siblings or I received our allowance we had to sit down with Mom to calculate how much we had earned. She wanted us to equate work with money so we would appreciate the amount of effort required to obtain a financial reward.

Each week she reviewed the chores that each of us completed, clarified the amount of pay for each task, and then calculated how much allowance we had earned. It was always very clear that if you wanted more money you simply did more work. Our allowance was never an entitlement.

After determining how much was owed, Mom would open her purse and count out the exact amount. The money was then divided into three different piles that contained 10%, 50%, and 40% respectively. The process was always the same. First we'd gather up the money in the 10% pile and place it into a church donation envelope. All six of us had our own box of church envelopes and I can clearly remember watching each of my siblings make their own contribution as the collection basket was passed each Sunday.

Next, we'd take the 50% pile and place it into an envelope to be deposited at the bank during the next trip to town. Mom had opened a savings account for each of us when we were eight years old so we could start saving for college.

CHAPTER 30 – SUCCEED BY SHARING

The remaining 40% was placed in a coin purse that was kept in an upper kitchen cabinet out of sight. We each had a handwritten paper inside our coin purse with the money.

Although we were allowed to make our own decisions about how we spent the money, we were responsible for documenting the expenditure so Mom could review what we purchased the next time our allowance was paid. The 50% I saved from my meager allowance and after school jobs was enough to pay cash for my entire first year of college.

Consistent contributions over time will produce a huge amount of money. My Dad earned less than $3000 per year when he first started his job at the oil refinery in my hometown of Mandan, North Dakota. He and Mom religiously (no pun intended) gave 10% to the church and saved 10% of their gross pay for retirement while raising six children. They never made an exception in thirty-five years other than to increase the amount they saved and donated. Their will power has always been an inspiration to me!

Initially, my parents' rate of savings was less than $1 per day, but each time Dad got a pay increase, they increased their savings accordingly. Over thirty-five years they amassed over one million dollars. You can do the same thing through consistent saving and discipline.

Share Your Time and Talent

My Dad was a jack-of-all-trades who worked many double shifts at the oil refinery to earn extra income. Many times he'd arrive home to find a kid, often not one of his own, waiting for him to weld the handlebars on their bicycle or fix their wagon or some other toy they'd broken. He had a heart of gold and could never say no, even if he was exhausted from working sixteen hours straight.

Change in Real Life

Sleepless Satisfaction

While in high school, I was overhauling the engine of my car in our garage and was having trouble getting the pistons back in the cylinders. Dad came home from work and stopped to see how I was doing before going into the house.

He started helping me and we pulled an all-nighter rebuilding the engine. The next thing we knew, Mom was telling Dad that it was time to go back to work. Imagine how tired he must have felt, but I know from experience that the personal satisfaction you receive from helping others will give you a burst of adrenaline that lasts for days.

Although we lived in the country, Mom made sure that we were involved in sports, band, 4-H, Boy Scouts (or Girl Scouts), and religious studies. She'd grown up on a farm and couldn't partake in many extra-curricular activities, but she was determined that her kids would not suffer the same fate.

She seemed to be continually dropping us off and picking us up from all the activities in which we were involved. She would often go out of her way to give our friends and neighbors a ride home too. When my youngest sister, Kelley started school, Mom got a job to help pay for all the band instruments, Scout uniforms, and sporting equipment. She also did the laundry for the nuns at the local convent in exchange for piano lessons for her children.

If you stop to think of all the volunteers you've benefited from throughout your life you'll be amazed. Val Heck was a scoutmaster for more than 20 years in my hometown and was directly responsible for at least twenty kids attaining the rank of Eagle Scout, including my brother and me. Many adults in the community also sacrificed their time to help each scout earn more that 30 merit badges.

Don Baker, who worked with my Dad, took time out of his life to lead our 4-H club. His daughter Lisa and her husband Frank Walter now live in Tucson within a few miles of us. They recently supported a fundraiser we held for the Make-A-Wish Foundation on my 50th birthday.

Everyone has skills and talents that could benefit others. Drive by any church, synagogue, or mosque to see what a focused group of individuals can do. Everything inside and out has been *donated!*

If you've ever been in Little League sports, taken swim lessons, been to summer camp, played in a park, taken college classes, or been on a class field trip, you've benefited from someone else's kindness. Don't you think it's time to "pay it forward" by using some of your time and money to help someone else?

SOLD ON CHANGE!

As a life-long learner, I try to surround myself with positive people. I read books that promote positive thinking. I have over 200 audio books in my library and listen to them in the car wherever I go. Many of my audio book purchases were recorded on cassette tapes. One of the reasons I still drive my 1999 Ford Expedition is that it has both a compact disc and cassette player.

A book that had a profound affect on me was "Seeds of Greatness" by Dennis Waitley. After reading the book I was compelled to complete the "wheel of fortune" exercise to determine how balanced my life was. By answering 24 simple questions about how satisfied you are with eight aspects of your life, you can create a circle chart to see where imbalances may lie. I was astounded to find that my level of community support had fallen very low, so I became determined to improve my score.

Shortly after completing the exercise, I began teaching a course on Personal Finance to sixth and seventh grade kids through the Junior Achievement program. My parents had done a fantastic job of educating me financially. In 1992, I began to pay it forward to other kids. Camille taught some of the classes with me when she wasn't volunteering at Children's Hospital in Dallas, TX.

When we moved to Tucson, AZ, Camille and I became involved with Montlure, a children's church camp that was struggling financially. During the six years on the Board of Directors (three years as its president) we substantially

increased the camp's income, improved the level of safety for
the campers, and left it far better than we'd found it.

In the past decade I've spent thousands of hours
creating real estate marketing pieces and tracking mechanisms
to manage our brokerage. Each year we hold seminars to share
what we've created with other real estate agents from around
the country.

At a recent training event attended by 42 agents we
were able to raise over $28,000 for the Make-A-Wish
Foundation in one day. In the day-long training event at a local
hotel, each Department Manager in our company gave a
presentation explaining how their department is set up, who
does each task, and how they track their output!

The day ends with a field trip to our main office and our
sales office to meet all the members of our team. Attendees are
allowed to visit with the people in each department and ask
any questions they might have.

You don't have to be wealthy in order to give. If you
don't have the financial resources, you can donate your time
and talent. The world is full of good people and everyone has
something of value to offer. If you're creative and willing to
share of yourself, others will follow; they just need to be
educated about the need. Many of the venues you approach
will discount or waive the cost of food and facilities when you
explain that it is for a charitable event. All you have to do is
ask!

Share Your Wealth

While growing up I can remember several times that another family experienced a hardship and my parents did something to help. Even though he had a family of eight to support, when Dad would hear about another family in need he'd tell Mom, "We should send them some money." They always gave what they could.

Although we live in a world of plenty, and have an abundance of everything, many people have the illusion that there is a shortage of money and you must conserve it at all costs. Most people are so focused on conserving their money that they never see opportunities to *earn* more.

Change in Real Life

Take Time to Make a Difference

For my 50th birthday in 2009, I set an aggressive goal of raising $50,000 for the Make-A-Wish Foundation. With the help of many friends and staff members, our 50/50 party was a complete success.

Although we didn't reach our goal during the one-night event, we surpassed it by the end of the year. By hosting the fundraiser and donating $100 for each foreclosed home we sold, our small company was able to grant the wishes of ten terminally ill children that year!

In extremely cold weather, the human brain will detect a reduction in your body temperature and constrict your blood vessels. This shuts down circulation to your limbs in order to conserve body heat for your vital organs. Unfortunately, the brain does the same thing when your financial outlook looks bleak.

Giving to charity changes your thought process. When you give something away, it sends a message to your brain that there is plenty to go around. This enables you to take advantage of new opportunities that you wouldn't have realized were there if your attention was focused on conserving or hoarding what you have. You must open your wallet to open your mind!

Most US business owners are subject to 30% or more in income tax and must pay an additional 15% in self-employment tax. The combined taxes on income account for nearly *half* of the money they earn! Most donations made to charitable organizations are tax-deductible, so whatever you contribute *really* costs about half of the amount you pay because the other half would be paid in taxes.

If the owners of a coffee shop pledge ten cents for every cup of coffee they sold it would only cost them five cents after taxes, but the charity would receive all ten cents of the donation. If the shop sold 300 cups of coffee per day, the charity would receive $30 per day, which would lead to $210 per week, $910 per month, and $10,920 per year!

If the coffee shop owners waited until the end of the year to give to the charity, they probably would not be able to pay $10,920 and if they could, the check would be very painful to write. Small amounts given consistently over time are virtually *painless* and can make a HUGE difference!

Recently, I was interviewed by a local television station at a Boys & Girls Club facility in Tucson, AZ. The entire facility, complete with gymnasium, computer lab, classrooms, and equipment had been donated, yet the facility had to cancel sports leagues and close the building a few days each month because of budget constraints. I asked the reporter, "Don't you think it's pathetic that such a magnificent gift is being wasted because a city of one million people can't raise enough money to pay the staff and keep the utility bills paid?"

If each Tucson resident would give just one dollar per month, we could raise twelve million dollars annually and could build several new clubs each year to keep more *at-risk* kids off the street. That's the trouble with society; everyone expects that someone else will step forward to give their time and financial resources.

Several of the top-producing real estate agents from across the country supported my birthday fundraiser. Many of the agents who attended also sold foreclosed homes and were interested in helping kids. Since banks refer to foreclosed homes on their balance sheet as "Real Estate Owned" (REO) we formed a group called REO4Kids.

Because foreclosures were having such an adverse affect on inner city kids, our REO4Kids group adopted Boys & Girls Clubs of America and began to donate $100 for each foreclosed property we sold. During the first three months of 2010, our small group of 18 agents raised an amazing $67,000 for children's charities.

We received national attention for our gift and were well on our way to achieving our annual goal of $250,000 when I had the idea of asking the financial institutions we worked for to *match* our contributions. If we were giving $100 to charity maybe they could too! Within a few hours of making the request, PMH Financial in Denver, CO agreed to do it!

If all of our clients could do that, we would double the $250,000 goal we set for ourselves. We determined that if we could recruit 100 members to the group we could give a million dollars *every year!*

There is magic in numbers when a group reaches that size. When a group of one hundred people comes together and focuses on the same goal, amazing things can happen. For every $100 each volunteer is able to raise or donate, $10,000 is raised for the charity. If each volunteer can raise $1,000, then the charity will receive $100,000.

The factor of ten works in reverse with expenses. To pay a $100 utility bill, each person only needs to contribute $1.00. Have you ever seen a bank *multiply* your income and *divide* your expenses by one hundred? That is what happens when a group of this size focuses on a charity. The best part is that nearly half of the amount contributed comes back to those who donate it as a tax refund.

Change in Real Life

<u>Give to Receive</u>

A few days after making our first quarter donation of $11,000 to the Boys and Girls Club in Tucson, AZ we were invited to a "Meet and Mingle" function at a local restaurant. I was pleased that each participant paid for their own food and drinks and did not use Club money for such functions.

We were introduced to several sponsors and those who served on the Board of Directors. A woman I'd been introduced to earlier approached me at the salad bar. After confirming that I was a real estate agent she said, "I think it's wonderful what you are doing for the Club. If you have the time to find ways to help others, you must have a well-run business. I'd like to list my home with you; can I call you tomorrow?"

The woman's home turned out to be valued at $400,000. With a 3% commission, we'd earn a commission of $12,000, one thousand more than we'd given a few days earlier.

<u>The Boomerang Effect</u>

I can attribute much of our business success to sharing with other real estate agents on the various forums. I never know who will benefit from my website posts on REObroker.com, NRBA.com, and CPCoaching.net but I take the time to explain new concepts or processes to my peers with the hope that they will benefit from my ideas and will share something in return.

CHAPTER 30 – SUCCEED BY SHARING

I can't count the number of times that people have approached me at conferences to tell me how much they've benefited from an idea I shared. These agents feel indebted to me and are always looking for ways to repay me for helping them.

I call this the *boomerang effect*. Although this is not the reason we give, it always seems to happen. When you give something away, a short while later you get back something that is greater than what you had. My Mom explains it like this, "You can't out-give God."

I always tell the agents who have benefited from my sharing to just "pay it forward" and help someone else, but they still look for ways to do something kind for me. I can attribute at least five of my REO account relationships to introductions by someone I helped with their business. Over the past few years, the relationships with bank clients I would not otherwise know have led to commission income of over *one million dollars!*

I'd like to challenge you to take the time to make a difference in someone else's life. It will reward you beyond belief, but you first must give without ever expecting anything in return. ***Pay It Forward!***

31

Modify
Your Mindset

Change your life by choosing like-minded friends who share with and challenge you

"I hope that my achievements in life shall be these - that I will have fought for what was right and fair, that I will have risked for that which mattered, and that I will have given help to those who were in need, that I will have left the earth a better place for what I've done and who I've been." – C. Hoppe

Surrounding yourself with a network of like-minded people will build a support group that can be instrumental in helping you achieve your goals. When the people in your group take action, it will give you the courage to do it too.

Public Proclamation

Our pride is a huge motivator to accomplish what we set out to do. Whenever I've taken on a challenging task, I tell everyone that I know what I plan to do.

Public proclamations are responsible for helping me to achieve many of my toughest goals. After telling everyone on my team that I would write this book in a *month*, I finished it in just 26 days. Holding yourself accountable works!

When you make a public proclamation, pay attention to how the people around you respond to the news. This is a good way of determining who your friends really are. Those who are small-minded or jealous of your accomplishments may be afraid that you're going to pass them in status.

They won't be supportive of your goals and will privately hope that you fail. Because these people have never had the courage to change their own situation, your success will make them feel like a failure.

Don't let these people get you down. Surround yourself with genuine friends who have positive attitudes and are supportive of your ambitions. True friends will help you to succeed at your endeavors. Their encouragement will lift your spirits and increase your commitment to follow through and complete what you set out to do.

If you believe that there is a limited supply of anything, then a shortage might as well exist. The limit that exists in your mind is projected upon everything you see whether it's really there or not. You'll *never* grow your business if you don't believe that you can. Keeping an open mind will create unlimited possibilities.

Change in Real Life

Get a Coach

The average real estate agent spends a good deal of their time and money looking for customers. In the "information age" that we live in, I can't believe that there are still brokers who hand a new real estate agent a telephone directory and say, "start calling."

Since joining Craig Proctor's *Quantum Leap* coaching program <www.quantumleapsystem.com>, my wife and I have been able to totally transform our real estate business. We no longer *look* for customers; *they find us* because of the unique programs we learned to implement in our business.

During the housing market downturn from 2007 to 2010, our sales volume grew by 1,000%. We sold ten times more homes in the "bad" market than we were able to sell during the "good" market in 2005.

You need to work *smarter*, not *harder!* Find someone who's done what you want to do and ask them for help. Whatever they charge will be well worth the money, it certainly was for us!

SOLD ON CHANGE!

In order to learn, you *must* make mistakes. Throughout this book, I've shared several of the mistakes we've made along the way. There's a big difference between theory and practice. How much can you learn from someone who has never done what you want to accomplish? I'd much rather be *shown* what works than instructed about what *should* work.

Periodically, we open the doors to our office to hold training events for other agents. A two-day class includes presentations by the division managers and other key employees in our company. The class ends with a field trip of our main office and sales office. One hundred percent of the money we collect from these training events goes to children's charities; in fact we ask participants to make their check payable to the charity!

Improving the lives of children has been my motivation for developing, teaching, and now writing about our successes and failures in this book. For more information about our upcoming training events, please send an e-mail to: event@win3realty.com.

Happy Home Selling!

Bob Zachmeier

INDEX
People, Products, and Entities

SOLD ON CHANGE!

INDEX

ABOUT THE AUTHOR

 Bob Zachmeier was born and raised in Mandan, North Dakota. His parents taught by example that determination and a strong work ethic could achieve almost any goal.

As the third of six children, Zachmeier learned early in life to become self-reliant. At the age of sixteen, he owned a fireworks business, complete with billboard and radio advertising. The business helped fund his college education and that of several of his siblings.

He became a part-time real estate agent in 2000 at the age of forty. In 2002, he was earning enough from real estate investments to leave his job and end a twenty-two-year career in the defense electronics industry. Since starting in real estate, he has gone from one sale every *four months* to a sale every *twelve hours!*

In 2004, Zachmeier and his wife, Camille, founded Win3 Realty in Tucson, Arizona. The name reflects their desire to create a win-win-win situation for their clients, the community, and the agents and staff in their company. They actively support several children's charities and in 2010 received the "Spirit of Philanthropy" award from the National Association of Fundraising Professionals.

By sharing his experiences and practical advice as real estate broker, coach, college instructor, author, and lecturer, Bob Zachmeier has helped thousands of people improve their financial well-being.

To learn more about Sold On Change™ systems and tools, visit the website www.soldonchange.com. To find additional titles by the author, including Upside Up Real Estate Investing™, visit the publisher's website at <www.outoftheboxbooks.com>. You can contact the author via e-mail at <bob@bobzachmeier.com>.

LaVergne, TN USA
30 January 2011

214526LV00007B/88/P